THE
CHURCH THAT
NEVER SLEEPS

Praise for the Dream Center and
The Church That Never Sleeps

"The Dream Center is a hard-hitting haven where lives are dramatically changed, and dreams are not only realized but actually come true!"

Dyan Cannon

Actress

"Pastors Tommy Barnett and Matthew Barnett have the key to the problems of inner cities in America. It is the answer to the abandonment by many of the churches to the suburbs and reaching of the lost in our inner cities. I commend them heartily for this ministry thrust into the heartland of America."

Paul Crouch

Founder, Trinity Broadcasting Network

"*The Church That Never Sleeps* is the story of one of the most remarkable ministries in the world today, and it is planted right in the middle of a war zone—downtown Los Angeles, California.

"The commander and shepherd of this incredible A-team of inner-city specialists is Matthew Barnett, one of the most courageous, selfless, and loving men I have ever met. He challenges our cold indifference and apathy toward the masses of broken, hurting, and self-destructive people in our own cities and shows us how to turn tragedy into triumph.

"*Caution:* This book will be harmful to indifference and passivity. It will awaken, challenge, and bring change to a boring life!"

Rick Godwin

Senior Pastor, Eagle's Nest Christian Fellowship

"The Dream Center is a cutting-edge ministry that is setting the trend for the church in the twenty-first century."

Josh McDowell

Author and Speaker

"The Dream Center . . . truly a place where dreams are rekindled by the grace of God."

Deion Sanders

Defensive Back, Dallas Cowboys

THE
CHURCH THAT
NEVER SLEEPS

MATTHEW BARNETT

THOMAS NELSON PUBLISHERS®

Nashville

Published in Nashville, Tennessee, by Thomas Nelson, Inc.

Library of Congress Cataloging-in-Publication Data

Barnett, Matthew.
The church that never sleeps / Matthew Barnett.
    p. cm.
ISBN 0-7852-6859-6 (pbk.)
    1. Los Angeles International Church (Los Angeles, Calif.) 2. Los
Angeles (Calif.)—Church history. 3. Barnett, Matthew. I. Title.
BX8765.5.Z7 L673 2000
289.9′4′0979494—dc21

                                                                99-053145
                                                                CIP

Printed in the United States of America.

3 4 5 6   05 04 03 02 01 00

This book is dedicated to every person who has given his life for the greatest calling known to mankind. To all of those who've agonized over a dream and to all of those in the trenches who work so hard and receive so little praise, keep going and continue to be courageous in your work in helping the outcast, for great is the God in you.

To my mother, who has given me an example that still inspires me to this day, I owe special thanks for all the wonderful talks and the courage you've given me to stand.

To my dad, I'm thankful you're my father, but I owe greater thanks to you for being my best friend. You have shown me how to "overdose on life."

To Luke, thanks, big brother, for showing me what perseverance means and for being so loyal to your little brother.

To Kristie, I love you. Sis, thank you for demonstrating to the world the power of joy. It is contagious, and whenever I'm blue, I think of your sweet smile.

To Caroline, my wife, you are the love of my life and the woman of my dreams.

To Todd, you are my foremost armorbearer. Thank you for helping me write this book "ghetto style."

To all of the Dream Center pastors, staff, and congregation who have stirred a nation by your commitment to your city, you have given and given, then you've given more. I love all of you so much. I make a promise to serve you all the years of my life as your pastor. Just thinking about you is inspiring to me.

To all the churches of America that have supported us and the special pastors who have believed in us from the beginning, we are here because of you.

CONTENTS

FOREWORD

As I READ the early chapters of the book of Acts, I am struck by the unusual nature of the church at Jerusalem. These early believers were driven by an intense love for Christ that expressed itself in the most dramatic demonstrations of selflessness. The joy of seeing hurting people blessed overcame intense persecution, and the gospel of Jesus Christ exploded from this city into the whole Roman world. One congregation provided the seed to change the lives of millions.

In all my travels, I have not seen a place and people so reminiscent of Jerusalem as the Dream Center, the Los Angeles International Church. The love of Christ is transforming the lives of hurting people, the most desperate and broken people to be found in our culture.

Pastor Matthew Barnett has begun a true revival with a fountain of love that heals prostitutes, drug addicts, gang members, and derelicts of every kind. Little children are touched by the thousands and are given the hope they need to rise above a hopeless environment.

The Dream Center is a place where people rise from the depths to soar in life. It is a vision that brings out the very best in God's people and demonstrates daily that no matter how great the ravages of sin, the grace of God is always greater.

The book you are about to read will change your life. You will catch something of the excitement and passion for souls that drove the early church disciples to the ends of the earth. You will see the misfits of society in a different light. You will find a love in your heart for the most unlovely people around you.

This is the miracle of the Dream Center, the church so consumed with God's love that it never sleeps. It is John 3:16 incarnate: "For God so loved the world, that he gave his only begotten Son, that whosoever believeth in him should not perish, but have everlasting life" (KJV).

Pastor Willie George
Church on the Move
Tulsa, Oklahoma

INTRODUCTION

IT WAS A BEAUTIFUL DAY. A twenty-year-old evangelist was driving through the streets of Los Angeles. As he passed the historic Angelus Temple and drove through the streets of Echo Park, God laid a vision on his heart that someday he would pastor a church in Los Angeles. The time was forty years ago and the man was Tommy Barnett.

Thirty years later, God would lay the same vision on my heart. It was a hot summer night in Phoenix, and I was outside, lying on the hood of my car. God showed me a map of the United States and pinpointed Los Angeles. Then I knew that I would go to LA and build a church. I had no idea how it would happen, but I knew that I would be in LA someday.

Five years after that, my vision became a reality. At the urging of the Assemblies of God, my father and I went to Los Angeles. My father did not need another job. He was already pastoring a church of more than fourteen thousand members in Phoenix, Arizona. Yet my dad loves a challenge. I was never the first choice for a pastor. My father had lots of people in mind. But no one wanted to accept the job. When my father finally asked me if I would do it, I could not believe my ears. I had never pastored for one day in my life. But I remembered the vision that God had given me.

So, we went to Los Angeles. But God had laid still another dream in my heart—the twenty-four-hour church.

This dream has been the driving force behind the success of the Dream Center. When you have a dream, it tends to pull you out of yourself into another, greater self.

I used to ask my dad why convenience stores, supermarkets, and hospitals stay open twenty-four hours a day while churches are open only on Sundays and for a few hours on Wednesday. What if someone needs help in the middle of the night? If he has nowhere to go? Nowhere to sleep? No food to eat?

I knew that the church needed to be open twenty-four hours a day as well. But how could that be carried out? Who would run it? Where would you get the food to feed the hungry? Where would you get the clothes to clothe the needy?

In Los Angeles, we moved into the old Bethel Temple, the first Assemblies of God church that was birthed out of the Azusa Street revival in the early 1900s. The church was once the focal point of a nationwide revival, but over the years the ills of the inner city took their toll. The church lost its prominence as poverty settled on the streets, and the church was unable to adjust to the changing environment.

Our church began to do street outreach immediately. Finding a need and filling it is the philosophy by which my father and I have lived our lives. So we fed the hungry, clothed the unclothed, helped the hurting, and set out to change the destiny of the city. We discovered that Bethel Temple wasn't large enough to house people and to accomplish the goal of the twenty-four-hour church that could satisfy the needs of the community at any hour of the day or night.

Then one day, I learned that the Catholic Church had the old Queen of Angels Hospital up for sale. It had been one of the largest hospitals in the city of Los Angeles. The administrators had decided to make the move to a brand-new building about a mile away.

I took my dad to look at the property, and reminded him of my dream of the twenty-four-hour church. The old hospital was in terrible shape. It would take a lot of work to make any part of the facility usable. Water was several feet deep on many floors because of flooding. Window-panes were missing; walls were damaged; trash was everywhere. It would take a miracle to restore the dilapi-dated building.

My father embraced the idea of trying to raise funds to purchase the 400,000-square-foot facility. The initial asking price was $16 million. Through a miracle of God, we were able to purchase the entire property for only $3.9 million with $500,000 down.

Because of unbelievable financial miracles from churches and individuals all across America and around the world, the building is now completely paid off and is undergoing extensive renovation.

Those first few months in the building, we spent most of our time cleaning. To this day, we are renovating floors of the fifteen-story hospital so that they can be actively used for helping hurting people. We have a group of people committed to getting this massive project done. Many are full-time volunteers who live and work on the campus, giving up a year of their lives to work for God. Others are broken people who are being rehabilitated to help them rejoin society.

Today, the Los Angeles International Church, also known as the Dream Center, is home to hundreds of people. We have two hundred ministries that reach out to the community, and people have come from all over the world to volunteer here.

And my dream has become a reality because the Dream Center is always open—twenty-four hours a day, 365 days a year. The staff and volunteers feed, clothe, and disciple people and go out every day into the dangerous streets of LA to share the message of hope and meet the needs of people. The list of services goes on and on:

- More than forty services are held each week with ten ethnic churches in multiple languages.

- More than ten thousand people are fed weekly through our food truck.

- More than one thousand articles of clothing are distributed monthly through our free clothing store.

- More than one hundred men and women stay in our Discipleship Home as they break addictions to drugs and alcohol and learn to serve the Lord.

- The Teen Reach youth home ministers to troubled teens twenty-four hours a day.

- Hope for Homeless Youth ministers to the thousands of outcasts who live in abandoned buildings and on the streets: street dwellers, prostitutes, and young people who've lost hope after coming to Hollywood in search of a dream.

- A free twenty-four-hour-a-day medical clinic is open at the Dream Center.

- The home for unwed pregnant women will start shortly.

My dream is to bring in as many ministries as possible and network with them and allow the Dream Center to be the base of operation for citywide outreaches. Every one of our ministries caters to a different need in the city. By allowing them all to come here and minister from this place, we can touch everyone in the city, rich or poor.

Through all of the various ministries and a committed army of inner-city volunteers, my dream has become a reality. I now proudly serve at the LA International Church—the church that never sleeps.

1

Whataburger Nights

It was 6:45 p.m. The church service was starting. I was pulling into the massive parking lot with my mom. A little boy, timid, shy, and scared of his own shadow, I jumped out of the car and headed for the large building. The Arizona sunset was quite impressive, and a beautiful church surrounded by mountains boldly faced me as I walked up to the building. It was always a nice walk from the parking lot to the church building. I made the same journey every Sunday night past the green grass, the magnificent water fountains, and the lovely stained glass picture of Jesus holding out His hands with a look of great compassion, followed by an arrangement of colorful flowers.

I entered the church as I had done hundreds of times and didn't realize how amazing my journey from the car to the church was. It was not a typical church, but what did I know? I was used to it. I sat down in a pew near the middle of the lower floor, totally unaware of the massive edifice and the thousands who gathered every week. I waited for the waterfall curtain to rise fifty feet in the air, and when it did, I sang along with the three-hundred-member choir. That was my life, and that was how I was raised, a pastor's son in a megachurch.

At 7:45 the preacher started his message, and once again my father delivered a powerful sermon, which received an enthusiastic response from the congregation. Then at the end he asked those who wanted to receive Christ as their personal Savior to come down to the front, and boy, did they ever! Hundreds made their way to the front to give their hearts to the Savior every week. Rich, homeless, middle class—all felt welcome to receive love from God and a prayer of hope from their pastor.

The service was over and the crowd filtered out of the auditorium, but there was my dad, still talking to the last person left in the auditorium. I knew he was tired. I could see it in his eyes as he tried to keep a smile on his face and express interest in every need. Only a son could tell he was tired and wanted to go home, but he was on a mission to love people and care for their needs.

My father and I had a little ritual when I was a boy. Every Sunday night after the service was over, we went to a hamburger joint called Whataburger, and we talked about life. Although he had just finished talking to what seemed like the entire congregation, my father always had energy to listen to me. I loved my father for many reasons that others in the church did not know. We didn't have to talk about religious things. Very rarely did we. He was just my friend, my pal, the greatest buddy that I had.

Those nights at Whataburger were nights of my discipleship, training, and comfort that would give me the foundation for what I would need years later. My dad thought that I was a funny boy because I asked some of the strangest questions. It seemed that there was an unwritten rule between us that said, "Matthew, you can ask any question that you want." And I did.

As the years passed, I became a teenager, but we still shared those Whataburger nights. Although I was more independent and liked to go out with my teenage friends, I could not get enough of those Whataburger nights with Dad. Our conversations were more in depth. We talked about the future, dreams, and goals, and what I would do with my life.

The idea of being a pastor was far from my mind, and I kept it that way. My reason was summed up in one word: *fear*. Why would anyone want to follow in the footsteps of a man who will go down in history as one of the great men in the world of Christianity? I felt that whatever I did, however hard I worked, I would always be measured by the success of my father, so I decided to do something else with my life.

I realized that my life was good. I didn't rebel against being a pastor's son by running around with girls, getting drunk, or dabbling in drugs. No one is perfect, but I didn't go that direction. In fact, I always loved God, and I can't think of a Sunday I missed going to church even during the rocky years of teenage life. Many pastors' sons tell horror stories about their dads never being at home or the pressure of being a pastor's son. But I never felt that way or saw my lot in life in a negative way. I liked almost everything about my life. It was comfortable and a nice way to be raised.

I always had a feeling that God would do something unique in me. I never felt that it would be working for God in the ministry, but I felt that in some way something big would happen that would change my life forever. Have you ever felt like that? As if someday soon something is going to happen that will dramatically change you forever? It's a feeling that life will be turned upside down, or things will go in a new and exciting direction.

CAMP AND MY NEW DIRECTION

It was the month of June, time for church youth camp. I was fifteen years of age. I packed my bags and could not wait to get to the mountains of Colorado. My thoughts were on many things. Most of them, to be honest, did not concern God. I thought of friends, sports, contests, the freedom of being away from home, and yes, girls. I loved everything about youth camp except the night services, which were boring to me. We sang for an hour, then we heard a preacher talk for an hour, then everyone cried for two hours at the front, and we went back to our rooms late at night. However, I could tolerate it because we had a lot of fun the rest of the time. It's not as if I didn't love God. I just felt that I needed a break from church.

The service had gone according to formula the first two

nights, singing, preaching, kids going to the front wanting to change their lives and turn back to God, weeping and crying out to God. That part was always impressive. Some kids, who were hard and rebellious, humbled themselves and pledged to God to walk the straight and narrow. It was a familiar sight to me. That was not the first time I'd seen the power of God in action.

On the third night, I decided to really listen to the camp speaker. I don't remember exactly what he spoke about, but I think he was speaking about what you can do when you have the power of God in your life. His message was short, and as I listened, I was amazed at how passionate he was about what he was saying. He was on fire! I think his zeal for God put me in tears before the altar call began. He gave the invitation for those to come to the front who wanted that power in their lives. I walked down the aisle, he prayed for me, I fell to my knees, and I didn't get up until five hours later. I don't know if anyone prayed for me that night. If someone did, I couldn't remember because I was off in my own world. Faith flooded my soul, a love for people came over me, and I knew that when I walked out of that room at 2:00 A.M., the old chapter of my life was complete, and a new Matthew Barnett was ready to come forward.

I walked out of that little chapel tucked away in the mountains, and everything looked different: the stars, the trees, and life in general. That night, something happened to me that was very special. My heart was turned toward a desire to work for God. I saw no great vision; I heard no life-changing word. But I was willing to say, "Whatever You want, God, I'll do it."

I wanted to go back home and tell the world what God had done in my life.

I returned home and shared my experiences with my dad at Whataburger. He was overjoyed, and he could tell my passion was real. At church services, I didn't sit in the back. I sat on the front row. When my dad preached, I preached right along with him, "Amen! Preach it!"

I can honestly say I knew God for myself, and it was great. After my camp experience, I loved to be with God. Every night I walked somewhere and prayed for two hours. I cannot even begin to tell you how special those nightly prayer walks were.

I put that fire into action too. Every Sunday night I went to the inner city of Phoenix, picked up homeless people, and took them to church. Every Saturday I went to the housing projects and picked up the little kids from single-parent homes and took them to church. Working for God consumed my life, and I enjoyed every minute.

GOD'S PURPOSE FOR ME

One hot summer night, I was lying on the hood of my car in Phoenix. At age sixteen, I was thinking about my future. I received a vision from the Lord that showed me a city in need. God put that city in my mind over and over again; it was the city of Los Angeles. Before when I thought of Los Angeles, I thought of Disneyland, Universal Studios, and Beverly Hills. I didn't think about inner-city Los Angeles. I never thought about ministering to gangs, prostitutes, or people in housing projects, so the dream had to be from God.

The vision showed me that someday I would be in Los Angeles and pastor a church in the heart of the city. I wrestled with God as Jacob did at Jabbok. But in the end God won. He always wins, but when He wins, we win. I surrendered my will that night and realized that whatever He wanted me to do, I'd do it. I said, "God, I will preach the gospel." I didn't know when I would be in Los Angeles, but I told God that I would start preaching in churches, youth groups, anywhere that gave me a chance.

At age seventeen, I started speaking at churches all over Arizona. Small country towns, truck stops, Native American reservations—you name it, I'd preach there. I drove four hours to speak at one church with twelve members in Springerville, Arizona.

Then God opened up other doors, and I preached in many states. I flew across the country, speaking in large crusades and youth conferences and having a good time. It was the kind of life I liked. I was young, I had money in my pocket from offerings, and my calendar was full for one year in advance. It seemed to be the direction of my life, and I made the best of the opportunity. I really felt that it was what I would be doing with my life, and Los Angeles was far from my mind.

When I was in high school, every year during summer vacation I stayed in Kansas City with my grandmother and preached at different churches that she lined up for me in the area. Every morning, I went to the little field by her house and prayed. During the summer of my senior year, I couldn't shake an uneasy feeling. I felt that something was going to happen, and I wouldn't be doing what I loved to do much longer. I had gone through so many changes in the last few years, it was hard for me to believe that I would go through another. I wasn't as excited about being on the road, and I seemed to have lost the desire. I wanted to be excited, but I couldn't.

The door of opportunity quickly closed for me, and I didn't go around knocking on it either. Was God shutting me out? Was He mad at me? Whatever it was, I was confused and didn't like it. Months went by and my calendar was empty. Churches were not calling, and I found myself on Sundays right where I used to be, on the front row of my father's church.

It felt strange to be so busy, flying here and there, feeling needed, and all of a sudden, back into church as I was when I was a youngster. With all of my free time, I found myself asking questions of my father at our same old hamburger joint on Bell Road. He was always kind and understanding and offered comfort and assurance. I realized that if everything in the world fell apart, I would still have those special Whataburger nights with my father. I gained great wisdom from him about how to deal with success and failure because he told me of all his ups and downs. Whenever I felt down, he told me of a young man who felt the same way, and he was always that young man.

At that time I didn't know what was going on, but God had done something very special in my later teenage years. What He was doing I did not see then, but now I do. He was knitting our hearts together for a reason. My season of travel was over. It was time to get back to a season of discipleship with my father at Whataburger. Almost everything else stood still for a while, but my relationship with my father kept growing. Thank God, it did because soon I would need that relationship. My life was about to undergo a drastic change.

2

You're Not in Phoenix Anymore

MY FATHER RECEIVED a call one day from a top official in the Assemblies of God denomination. He said that he wanted to speak to him because he had a very important challenge for my father. He flew out to Phoenix like a man on a top secret mission ready to lay out his case point by point. Now you have to understand that my father didn't need any more projects. He had built one of the largest churches in America with more than fourteen thousand members, and the top official knew that, but decided to give it the old college try.

My father was fifty-six years of age at that point and was thinking about pastoring the Phoenix church, buying a house in beautiful Flagstaff, Arizona, and settling down. At least, my father told the family that, but we never believed him. He has always been a man with great vision and passion for ministry. In other words, he loves a challenge.

The representative from the denomination told my father horror stories of what had become of the church in the inner city, using Los Angeles as a model. Most of the

11

churches in our denomination and other denominations had left the inner city for greener pastures and more money in Orange County. One by one, the stories were told, and my father was left with one big fact: "The city of Los Angeles needs a great church." But not just another church—a new kind of church that would set America on fire. My father listened kindly but made no commitment, and the gentleman left. He tried to push it aside; however, the desire wouldn't leave my father.

Along with pastoring, my father spoke at churches across the country. His schedule was always busy as he challenged pastors and congregations to make a difference in their communities. His trips frequently took him to southern California. With every visit, he got into his car and drove to downtown Los Angeles (his favorite place), drove by the old Angelus Temple, where Aimee McPherson pastored, and Azusa Street, the site of the powerful revival in the early 1900s. He loved the city so much.

When he returned to Phoenix, he couldn't get the city of Los Angeles out of his mind. He wrestled with the idea of starting a church until he knew that it was time to act. He called the denominational official and told him that he would explore the possibility of starting an inner-city church in LA.

As a family, we were aware of the cost to every member to see this thing work. We all knew that once Dad decided he would "take a look," more than likely, our lives were about to dramatically change.

My father had always dreamed of pastoring a church in a big city with racial diversity. However, this was different. This was the inner city, not suburban Phoenix. The streets were cold and dark, and gangs surrounded the communities. Life there didn't resemble life in comfortable middle-class Phoenix. It was, in reality, a wild dream for a well-respected man, who was known nationally, to go to a poor ghetto and want to start something for inner-city people. They had nothing financially to give him. It certainly wasn't safe or easy. He couldn't build the church on reputation. Most of the people were from the Third World. But love knows no boundaries and no limitation. Love isn't rational and doesn't always make sense. Your heart is connected with a group of people, and when that happens, you'll give anything for them.

Bethel Temple

In early 1994, my father planned a trip to LA to see the city and to visit the church that was being made available to him. I asked if I could join him. The Assemblies of God had offered my father the old Bethel Temple building, famous for being the first Assemblies of God church birthed after the Azusa Street revival. The revival sparked the pentecostal movement. Once the most influential Christians in Los Angeles attended there. By the 1970s, it was an old building in a poor, gang-infested neighborhood.

My father and I arrived in Los Angeles at night, and we

headed past the modern buildings of downtown. We drove toward Sunset Boulevard, just a mile away from the tall buildings of downtown. I thought Sunset Boulevard was going to be beautiful with palm trees lined up and down and modern shopping centers. Instead, I saw old buildings, shops with signs in various languages, and a filthy street.

We turned left on Marion Street, and there was the church. It was in the middle of a dimly lighted residential community. The church looked more like a museum than a church. We parked on the street and walked to the front entrance.

A group of young gang members looked at us rather suspiciously, as if to say, "What are you white boys doing here?" They were huddled together on the steps of the church and drinking beer. It was almost like a scene in the movies, a group of teenagers just "hangin' out in the 'hood." I was only twenty years of age, and I was terrified. I had never seen a group of gangsters up close and personal.

We entered the building and saw that, despite its age, it was very charming. It still had the ancient red theater-style seats. I was inspired about the possibilities of the church. Every step I took the floor creaked from years of wear and tear. I thought of all the history in that building. However, I was moved by an even greater thought, *What about all the possibilities for the future?*

I felt as if it were my home, and somehow I thought that I would return to the place. We toured the facility, then returned to Phoenix. The dream was in me. I wanted to pastor the church, but I never told my father of my dream because if it was God, He would open the doors and speak to my father's heart.

THE SEARCH FOR A PASTOR

After our visit to Bethel Temple, my father and I knew that a new church would start there. We talked it over with the family, and we all agreed that we ought to obey God and commit, as a family, to support the vision. My father would be the founder of the church and the spokesman nationwide. There was only one problem: Who would pastor the church?

We decided to list the top ten evangelists or pastors who had preached at my father's church in Phoenix and had dramatic effects upon the people. Then my father called them, explained the situation, and invited them to visit the church. One by one, they all expressed enthusiasm about the possibilities of pastoring in Los Angeles. Over the next few months they came to LA. However, when they saw the building, the neighborhood, their future, they declined and said, "Thanks, but no thanks." I'm sure it was hard for those men with established careers to think of settling down in the inner city with their families to pastor there. The job needed a pastor with nothing to lose, no wife or children, someone crazy enough to give it a try. Maybe some were called by God but did not respond. Or maybe none were called at all.

After looking long and hard, we could not find anyone to commit to pastoring the church. Having my father preach in two cities on the same day was not a realistic option.

Hundreds of people gather every Monday morning at my father's church to pray. It's a moving experience to walk into that building and hear the people crying out to God in the early morning hours. I owe much of my spiritual commitment today to those mornings of prayer.

One Monday morning, Craig Smith, a well-respected businessman in our church and a man my father loved like a brother, delivered a message to my father that he felt he received from the Lord. There could be no greater word of confirmation than one from your friend whom you admire greatly as a man of God.

Craig told my father, "Pastor, I know that you are looking for someone to pastor the LA church, and I've been in prayer about it. This might sound strange, but I feel that your son needs to pastor the church." My father expressed his surprise, but Craig continued, "I know he is young, but I know for sure that the Lord wants me to let you know that your son can pastor that church." Little did I know that my father, deep in his heart, always felt that, but he needed a confirmation. He got it from Craig.

My father came home and told me about what Craig had said and also what he had been feeling. I thought maybe my father wanted me to be his assistant (I was fine with that idea), but when he sat me down to talk to me, I knew he wanted something more. He wanted me to pastor the church.

To be honest, when he told me that he believed I could do the job, I didn't believe him. I always felt that I might pastor a church in Los Angeles someday, but not at twenty years of age and with no ministry experience. I could not argue, however; I knew that was my dream, my future, and my destiny, and I could not pass up what I knew to be my path. Was I scared? I was beyond scared. Somehow, though, I had the faith to take steps forward.

Looking back, I can't believe I was so blindly full of faith. I have found that God will let you see all the beauty of a dream at first and not scare you to death with all the pain that goes along with the beauty. Oftentimes, the heartache comes along as the journey continues. After living in shock for a while, I accepted the invitation to become the youngest pastor in the city and probably the nation.

Launching Out in Faith

A month later I was to preach. I didn't have time to prepare at all. Let me give you some idea of the challenges I faced. I had no ministry experience. I had not one day of pastoral duty. I was just a boy evangelist. I didn't know anything about a church budget. I couldn't begin to tell you how to run a board meeting.

The pastor I was to follow was eighty years of age and had been at the same church for twenty-five years. Pastor

Howard Barfoot had been faithful in his efforts and held the church together in the inner city. Although the membership was small, without him, I wouldn't have had the opportunity to pastor. He is a hero today to me because he wouldn't give up. He sowed much seed that has grown into the harvest of what God has done today through the Dream Center. But I'm getting ahead of my story.

I packed my bags in Phoenix ready to move away from home for the first time in my life. That was one of the hardest experiences of my young career. All of my life revolved around my family, and at one point all of my dreams were wrapped up in Phoenix. I was leaving my church, my lifelong friends, and my precious family.

As I drove down I-17, I drove by my life to that point, passing each place with a nostalgic feeling. I passed my high school and all the places I used to hang out on Friday nights. I appreciated all of those places more than I ever appreciated them before. My feeling was that I was starting life all over again, and I was. I thought the feeling would go away, but when I saw the sign that said, WELCOME TO CALIFORNIA, tears rolled down my cheeks. Reality set in: you're not in Phoenix anymore.

The closer I got to Los Angeles, the more terror flooded my soul. I wasn't quite as brave as I thought I was. It was time to be humbled. Driving through the neighborhoods, I got my wake-up call. Gang members over here, prostitutes over there, graffiti everywhere, and store signs were posted above run-down buildings in multiple languages.

It was quite a culture shock and a brief introduction to life in the inner city late at night.

I finally reached my new home in downtown Los Angeles. Buildings on every side, typical of downtown life, surrounded the apartment. They looked like giants to me, and in a strange way they were intimidating. Life had changed dramatically in a short span of time. The first thought that invaded me upon reaching the apartment was, *What am I doing here, and where is the freeway back to Phoenix?*

That night it seemed that I stared at the skyline of Los Angeles for hours, thinking about my life up to that point and where it was going. Everything inside me wanted to say, "Let's go home," as I agonized over the big task in front of me. But in the middle of my fears, the touch of God came heavy upon me and settled me. I unpacked my bags and prepared to undertake my new calling as pastor of the Los Angeles International Church, later to be called the Dream Center.

RAYS OF HOPE

The first few weeks were difficult. I was used to being around a large office with modern equipment and multiple staff members. A thriving megachurch was all I knew because I grew up in it. And I tried to get used to the silence. Sometimes a handful of staff helped me, but more often I was alone, except for the gang members outside on the steps. The thought kept popping up: *How in the world can I build a church under these circumstances?* The church was lacking energy, life, and resources.

The Sunday services were even harder. One barrier that I had to overcome was my inability to speak Spanish. I speak it almost fluently now, but at the time I could barely utter a word. The building seated eight hundred people, and maybe twenty-five people attended the services. Many didn't like the fact that they had a twenty-year-old inexperienced pastor.

Many times a few minutes before the Sunday night service, I looked out to check on the congregation, but no one was there. I scanned the parking lot for cars. Often, there were none. The sight of those empty spaces before a service scared me, and I couldn't seem to keep from crying. To make it worse, my father called me every Sunday night to ask me how the service went, and I acted as if everything were okay. But everything was not okay. I was failing. Those six months pushed me to the point of breaking.

In the middle of my difficult journey, I learned that God sends rays of hope along the way to keep you on the path. They might not be big rays, but the little rays that encourage you and enable you to go another day. For example, Gus Gabriel, an older Filipino pastor who had been with the church for twenty-five years, became my ray of hope. When the people became disgruntled with me as the new pastor, he visited all the members one by one and told them how and why they should support me. He has always loved me and has stood by me even when I made wrong decisions.

Without his courage behind me, my career would have ended a long time ago. He believed in me when I didn't believe in myself. He believed in me when the church wasn't growing. Today, now that the church is flourishing, he is still with me, cheering me on. It's true that when tough times come, you really find out who your friends are, and no man has proved his love for me like Amerigus Gabriel.

STRUGGLES WITHIN THE HEART

The church was not growing, and every night it seemed that I was weeping on the floor, wondering when the church would get going. I came from a big church, with big expectations, and I wasn't measuring up. I grasped for ideas, possible formulas, but nothing worked. I was no longer in Phoenix under the protection of Daddy. I felt I was all alone, and I thought I had to fight this battle for myself. But the battle was not in building the ministry. The battle was in the heart, for there every great dream is born.

3

PUTTING YOURSELF IN
ANOTHER MAN'S WORLD

MY FATHER ATTENDED a pastors' conference in the Midwest where a pastor stood up during a session and announced, "Early tomorrow morning, I'm going to tell every pastor what makes a great church." My father was so excited, he got up the next morning, found a front-row seat in the room, and got his notepad out. He was ready to hear the inspiring truth from the pastor. The pastor stepped up to the pulpit and said, "Let me tell you what makes a great church. One word, *trouble*." That's all he said. He closed his Bible and left the building.

I laugh every time I hear that story because that's the truth. Trouble allows every one of us to draw deep from inside and find out what we really believe. David said, "It is good for me that I have been afflicted" (Ps. 119:71 NKJV). Now he didn't say it *while* he was being afflicted. But after he had a chance to look back, he realized that the affliction made him what he was.

TESTING

Sometimes God will allow tough times to come at you immediately when you're following a dream because He wants to find out up front if you can withstand them. Most people who have accomplished great things for God testify to the same thing: their biggest test came in the beginning. I had many testings in the beginning, but one test was truly my most important.

For six months after I assumed my new pastoral duties, a group of young people from Phoenix helped me build the church. I used them in bus ministry, administration, and many other areas. They were my staff, and I knew that I could count on them. We worked together, struggled together, depended on one another. But one night, the young people decided that they had had enough and that they didn't want to be with me anymore.

They had a private meeting and discussed their future. All of them agreed that I wasn't doing a good job and that they needed to move on. I was saddened to learn about the private meeting, not just because the meeting was unethical, but also because they came to the conclusion that they didn't believe in me as a pastor.

I went home and cried on my pillow for three straight hours. It was the kind of cry that comes from deep within your gut, a cry that sometimes is needed to help you turn the next corner in your life. That kind of cry does one of two things. Either it makes you bitter at the world and you decide that you're not going to trust anyone, or it makes you better and something clicks inside that says, "I will *not* give up."

I have to say that cry was one of the best things that ever happened to me. A holy boldness came on me, a toughness that I never had before. While I was crying I pounded the ground and screamed out, "I will not give up! I will not give up!" After three hours, I wiped the tears and went back to work with a new attitude. It wasn't an arrogant attitude. It was a basic affirmation: "Everyone in the world can leave me, but I will not be moved." I was determined not to let the devil knock me down. A new fire was shut up in my bones, and I set out to build the church, no matter how hard and long I had to work.

REACHING OUT

I decided I was going to build the church the way I wanted to build it. But I knew it had to meet the people's needs, and I had to learn about those needs. Every night I explored my community. My mission was to integrate with my community. One night, I ate at a Mexican restaurant; the next day, a Chinese place; the next, a Cuban or Central American eatery. I walked through the parks and talked with the people in Spanish. I entered their world.

My life in Phoenix was history. I burned the boats behind me and never looked back. I didn't visit my family in Phoenix for a long time because I didn't want to get reattached as I had been. In a sense you could say that my loyalties were to Los Angeles and to my community.

Something special happened; my heart was knitted to the people. I left my world, and I put myself in their world. I ate what they ate, I worked among them, I visited their homes day and night, and I learned their culture. Too often in the church we expect people to come to our world. We build an establishment, and then we expect folks to come to our party. I've learned that to reach your community, you have to put yourself in another man's world.

Every week I made hundreds of house visits in the neighborhood, introducing myself as the new pastor and trying to build excitement about the church. At church services, I asked all the members to go out with me on Saturday and invite the people to come to our services. Most of the time no one accepted the invitation, so I went alone.

I wanted to get to know the people in my community so desperately that I put my desk and phone outside and did my office work in front of the church. As people walked by to take their kids to school, I said "Hi" to every one, hoping to build a relationship. I'd even throw in simple Spanish phrases: "¿Cómo estás?" (How are you?) or "Buenos dias" (Good morning).

It seemed that I went everywhere, trying to connect

with people. The church membership began to grow because of my efforts and the efforts of the church staff; we were determined to reach out to the needs of our community. We fed the people. We threw neighborhood block parties. You name it, we did it to build trust with the people. We gave away turkeys for Thanksgiving, presents for Christmas, and bags of groceries after services. We held contests and gave awards for those who brought the most people. We wanted to get people in the doors of the church, and it was working. People in the community were starting to come together. Funding came from people who saw the work we were doing and wanted to be involved.

After one year of ministry, I began to enjoy working in Los Angeles. Once I put myself in their world, I wasn't living for myself anymore. My concern was not with wondering what would become of Matthew Barnett, the son of the great pastor. My concern was with making life better for the people. Titles, influence, all of that was irrelevant and unimportant. It was just my people and me.

Many nights for fun, I went to the supermarket, bought all the groceries I could afford, and delivered them to families, just to surprise them. My visions were no longer of building big buildings. They were of helping individuals and making their lives better. Before God uses a person, it all begins in the heart. Once you catch it in the heart, the dream will unfold in front of your eyes.

Following Jesus' Example

In Matthew 26, one verse inspires me greatly. Let me set the scene. It was the end of Jesus' life. Only a couple of chapters are left before the gospel is completed. Jesus had only a few days left to live or maybe just a few hours before He would go to the cross—definitely the most important time of His life. If you had only a day or two left in your life, what would you do? I'm sure you would talk to a loved one, say good-bye to the family, or make things right with an enemy. Or you might want to do something that you've always been afraid to do.

So what was Jesus doing? With only a few hours left, shouldn't He have written a great doctrine, preached a farewell sermon, finished a book, or maybe given His disciples a final parting word? But the Bible says, "Jesus was in Bethany at the house of Simon the leper" (v. 6 NKJV). Jesus sat down to share a meal with Simon, who had sores all over his body and shedding skin.

We serve a God who showed us how to put Himself in another's world. He always looked for ways to serve others. In my opinion, that's what's needed in the church today. We have too many preachers who preach, but never minister to the hurts of the people. They preach a good sermon, leave the auditorium when church is over, don't shake hands with the people, and never go out to meet needs and minister to them in a personal way.

Many other times Jesus went out of His way to minister

to the needs of people. Jesus took the long way on His journey to an important feast and ministered to the Samaritan woman who was an outcast. Jesus entered Jericho, and a crowd gathered around Him. Yet He looked up to Zacchaeus, a nobody, in the sycamore tree and said, "Zacchaeus, I'm going to your house tonight and we're going to have dinner." He ate with the tax collector Matthew and said, "Follow Me." Even on the cross in the middle of His pain He told the thief next to Him, "You will be with Me in paradise." That's just who Jesus was, a man with a sincere love for individuals.

Following Jesus' example, the LA church began to grow, and it became a beehive of activity. I would like to say it grew because of my inspired and inspiring ideas, but it was simply growing by loving one person at a time. Then God sent various people and groups alongside who helped us and shared the same vision. With their help the church was filled every week.

Experiencing a Modern-Day Miracle

A miracle occurred in that neighborhood. It's amazing how a change in what we value can turn everything around. The first half of the year was awful, full of struggles for me. But with one change of focus, with the determination to love and serve people, the church turned around. Revival had come to that area.

A church member built a basketball court behind the

church and set up weights in the middle of an old dirt parking lot. It was a great idea! Every night hundreds of gang members and families came out to that court, played basketball, lifted weights, and ate dinner on the benches. We allowed some to spray-paint graffiti art with a positive message on our walls. Every night our small group of volunteers went outside after the office closed, and we lifted weights with the gang members, talked with families, and got to know everyone in the neighborhood. I couldn't believe that a dirt lot, with benches, weights, and basketballs, could do so much for that neighborhood. The church was packed, and community spirit came alive.

We seemed to spend all of our time finding ways to touch hurting people. We kept our doors open all day, and we allowed people to come in and pray, receive food, or seek other help. We wanted the people to claim ownership of the church. We built no fences to keep away troublemakers. We simply said, "Come." We invited everyone!

ESTABLISHING THE STREET DEACONS

My uncle donated the first bus we used for ministry. Soon, many others donated to the church. Our fleet now numbers sixteen buses.

From the beginning, we put the buses to good use. Basically the first church members were homeless people. In the beginning, 50 percent of the church came off the buses from skid row. Many lived in cardboard boxes. Boy, did those first members ever have personalities. We bused in nearly one hundred homeless people every service and gave them food afterward. I opened up the church to all, but they were the only ones who responded.

We created a program called Street Deacons. They were men from skid row who had been faithful in coming to church, so they were elevated and received the title of street deacons. The men had never been called anything but bad words in the past; they liked being given such a title. Their job was to bring in street people and keep peace on the buses. I praised them for doing a great job, and they thrived on the encouragement.

One of the deacons was named Figueroa, who was one of the biggest guys I've ever seen. He had muscles in every square inch of his frame. He was so determined to get people on the bus that he grabbed them and almost forced them to get on. The Bible says, "Compel them to come," but I think he sometimes took it a little too far.

FULFILLING NEEDS

When you put yourself in another man's world, you learn how to have vision. As Christians, we may think that to get vision, we have to go to a mountaintop somewhere and wait for hours for a revelation about what to do with our lives. Or we may feel that we have to go to a camp meeting or revival center to find out our purpose. But nothing of what exists today at the Dream Center was born out of a mountaintop experience. All of the vision was born in the valley. You see, in the valley we are close to the need. It's the place where we see the hurt. All of the Dream Center's two hundred ministries today were started by walking the streets, identifying with the people, and seeing the needs. After we saw a need, a vision came to fulfill that need.

Following one service, a homeless man came up to me and started weeping on my shoulder. He said, "Pastor, the sermon you preached gave me such hope, but tonight I have to go back to the cold streets and live with the temptations of drugs and alcohol. Can you find me a place to stay where I can live for God and get away from the streets?" I was saddened to have to tell him that I could do nothing for him. Tears rolled down his cheeks as he headed back to the streets of downtown.

I told God, "Someday I'm going to have a place where these men can stay overnight and be discipled." However, I would not have had that dream if it weren't for being in the valley and seeing the need. That is why in many areas the church is so out of touch with what is going on. Too many Christians live on the mountaintop of spiritual ecstasy, but fail to be happy. Why? Because we are happy only when we are giving. Just who are the happy people? They are the ones making a difference every week in the lives of others by living for others. If you live your life with palms up, you'll be happy only at Christmastime and your birthday, but if you live your life with palms down, you'll be happy 365 days a year.

After one year of pastoring the church, things were really looking up. Bethel Temple was packed every Sunday, which was something that hadn't been accomplished in decades, and the community was catching on to the vision. We had few resources, but we used whatever we had for ministry. Bethel Temple owned some houses in the neighborhood, and we allowed some of the men and women who wanted to be helped to live in those houses. In fact, ten houses were filled with men and women being trained to overcome their addictions and live for God.

The church was full; the houses were full; we had no more room to grow. During those first months in Los Angeles, I thought that it would take a lifetime to fill the old building. If you had asked me about my dream, I would have told you that it was to fill the building in the next ten years. But after one year, it was time to move to bigger quarters.

When I was in love with the idea of building church attendance, nothing worked. The church didn't grow. When I fell in love with people and meeting their needs, everything prospered and grew. Better than having ideas, better than coming up with church growth concepts, getting out there in the trenches, giving your life for people, is the best seed for a harvest.

When I got to the place in my life that I was in love with individuals, not accomplishments, the transformation led to prosperity. My dream is that all over America, churches will become excited about ministering in practical ways to the hurts of people. That is what it's going to take to bring about the next great move of God. Put yourself in another man's world.

BEING THERE

This story explains exactly what I'm talking about. Within a day after I arrived in Los Angeles, a young man was shot and killed in a drive-by shooting. His body lay near the steps of the church that I was about to pastor. Paramedics who were trying to revive the young man surrounded his lifeless body. It was useless; he was dead—another young man killed on the streets of Los Angeles.

That Wednesday night, only five or six people showed up for my first service. While I was introducing myself as the pastor, someone told me what was happening. I stopped my message and told my new congregation of what had happened across the street. I knew something had to be done, so I received an offering from the small group and told them that I'd return soon.

I went across the street with a little bit of money, terrified of the scene. I knocked on the door of the old apartment, and when I did, a big gang member with tattoos covering his arms opened it. He asked, "What do you want?" I said, "Just to let you know that I'm the new pastor in town. This is my first day. I want to let you know that I'm here to serve your family. Here's an offering from the church to let you know that we want to help." He looked at me as if to say, "You're the craziest white boy I've ever seen." But instead, he told me to come in.

I walked in with one objective: find the mother, give her the money, and leave as fast as I could. It was not hard to find the mother. She was crying hysterically at the loss of her son. Some of the gang members were trying to comfort her, but she was nearly punching them, not wanting anything they had to give her. In her eyes, they were the ones responsible for the death of her son. I felt so sorry for her.

Nearly shaking, I walked up to her and told her I was the new pastor, and we wanted to give her some money as a token of our love. She accepted graciously, and I was out the door. All of a sudden, the biggest gang member I had even seen in my life grabbed me by the arm and spun me around. I looked up at him, and he looked down at me. I looked up to God and said, "I've always heard about a place called heaven. Save a place for me. I'm coming home." I thought I was a dead man.

The fellow said, "I want you to stay and pray for us." At that moment I would have done anything he asked me to do. I stayed and prayed. We joined hands in a circle, and I started to pray a general prayer: "God, send Your peace on this family." However, something came over me, and the boldness of the Lord consumed me. I said, "Lord, I pray that because of this tragedy, not one of these young men will be in the gangs anymore, and they will come to know You." The grip on my hand got tighter, so I thought maybe he didn't like my prayer. The grip on my other hand got tighter as well. I thought, *I might not live much longer, so I might as well give it all I've got*. I prayed more boldly, and as I did, my hands were raised in the air with the gang members on my right and on my left as if to say, "We are with you." It was such a dramatic scene, Hollywood couldn't have written a better script. But it was real life. I then led them in the sinner's prayer, and they prayed and accepted Christ into their hearts.

From that moment, I had the best bodyguards in Los Angeles. After that day, peace seemed to sweep across our community. The young men became my friends. I look back now, and it's rather humorous that God would use me—as terrified as I was—to help those gang members. It doesn't add up or make sense. I've learned, however, that you can't fight love. It is still the most powerful force of all.

4

THE CHURCH I ALWAYS DREAMED OF

MY FATHER DID SOMETHING very wise for me when I was a youngster. He never discouraged my dreams. No matter how crazy they were, he let me speak what was in my heart. Growing up, I asked many questions, so many that I almost drove my parents to distraction. However, I believe that God speaks through people and gives them dreams at a young age for a purpose.

Throughout the Bible, the Lord spoke to young men regarding their future: to David when he received the anointing from Samuel; to Jeremiah when he was called to preach; to John the Baptist when he was anointed in the womb of Elizabeth. Many young people reach their dreams because growing up, they are encouraged to speak whatever their dreams may be. Usually people become what they are encouraged to become. You need to listen to the dreams of young men and women because there might be an anointing on their lives.

One question in particular that I used to ask my father was, "Dad, do you think that it's possible to build a church that would be open twenty-four hours a day?" My father replied, "I've never heard of something like that, but why don't you become the first person to build it?" I believed that with God's help I could do anything; nothing seemed impossible. Even as a young boy, I was already thinking about building this kind of church. If my father had discouraged my crazy dreams, I don't know where I would be today. But thank God, he didn't.

Someone on Your Side

I played sports year-round. At every game my father was there, which was amazing because he was so busy with pastoring, but he rarely ever missed a practice or game. Every year he won an award as "Fan of the Year." Every time I looked at him I felt as if I could win or I could make it. When I wrestled, there were many times that I was on my back ready to lose the match, but I could hear my father's voice. Somehow I felt as if it gave me an extra edge over my opponent. I was not wrestling alone. I had someone to believe in me.

No matter how tough life is, no matter how alone you are in building a church, running a business, penniless, friendless, or whatever, if you have just one person that you know believes in you, you can make it in this life. If you have just one idea, one dream, and you never let it die, there will be a day in which everything will somehow come together. Something will work in your favor, and one day you'll realize that the impossible is possible.

Some people don't give up on the journey. They keep going when others give up, and because of their incredible endurance, they see the fulfillment. I love this statement: "Great men are ordinary men who never give up." It's the truth. Dreamers are ordinary people who hang in there long enough to see the light at the end of the tunnel. How many great dreams are not being fulfilled in the world today because of people who lose heart, wash out, and give up? The Bible says, "We count them blessed who endure" (James 5:11 NKJV). That is, those who stay in the battle find great joy; quitters don't know what joy is. A dream lifts you out of yourself into another self, which is greater than yourself. My dream has inspired me to never lose hope. It keeps me going when I want to quit.

NINE ACRES OF DREAMS

During our great growth at Bethel Temple, I knew that we couldn't be there much longer. The residential community was not prepared for thousands of people coming to the church during all hours of the week. We outgrew the place in slightly more than a year.

One day, I was driving on the famous Hollywood freeway looking for buildings. Just two miles from Bethel Temple, there on the right side of the freeway was an enormous building. I pulled off the freeway out of curiosity and found a hospital in the middle of a large residential community. Houses and apartments surrounded it, making it look out of place. I later learned that the building had been empty for nine years.

I parked my car at the entrance of the hospital and walked around the place. I couldn't believe that such an impressive complex was vacant. There were nine acres of property, a fifteen-floor hospital building, and six other large buildings attached.

When I first thought of a new building, I had a typical church building in mind. The idea of a hospital didn't occur to me. However, I was intrigued by the possibilities of the site.

As I walked around, I noticed a security guard there, the only person on the property. I told him that I was interested in the building. He was rather hesitant at first, but he agreed to let me go in. He showed me through a few doors and left me to explore on my own. Was it ever an exploration. The floors were dirty, the lights were broken, graffiti was on the walls, and old medical files were scattered on the floors.

For decades, the hospital cared for the needs of the people. The dream for Queen of Angels was born in 1925 in the heart of a Franciscan sister of the Sacred Heart. The group of nuns built a hospital the hard way, by the sweat of their brows. They built it on a dream of helping the less fortunate and the truly needy.

For more than sixty years, that dream was a reality. Many people in our neighborhood were born in the hospital. It was strange to see an empty shell that had helped so many people. All of these thoughts raced through my mind.

Another thought consumed my mind as well: *Can these old bones live again?* All of the pieces came together in my mind, and I realized that it was the fulfillment of the dream that had been with me most of my life. The questions I asked my father at Whataburger, the dream of the twenty-four-hour church, the fulfillment of "the church that never sleeps."

My thinking began to change while walking from floor to floor. Suddenly my thoughts shifted from wanting to find a church building to wanting to find a place to build people. I thought, *On the fifteenth floor we can take in runaway kids. On the fourteenth floor we can take in unwed pregnant women.* It doesn't cost anything to dream, so I continued. I walked down every floor, declaring my dream for it. I saw a medical floor where we could minister to the sick in our neighborhood and another floor where volunteers from all over America could work with inner-city people.

I walked from building to building, and it was easy to piece the dream together. In two hours, I realized that the 400,000-square-foot hospital in the center of the city could be used to house the homeless, feed the poor, serve the community, and be a light for the city. It could be a place where people could volunteer for a week or a month, going into the streets and serving the poor. It could be a church that would be open seven days a week, twenty-four hours a day, to reach hurting people. It could be a place where a hurting family that needed food or clothes could come at any hour and be cared for, a place that would shower the city with love.

CASTING THE VISION

Something special was taking place in my heart. As a twenty-year-old pastor, I saw the place that would be home to the vision God had planted in my heart as a young boy. It would be a church similar to the early church of the book of Acts. My heart was beating so fast, I couldn't keep up with it. God showed me my future and what I was supposed to do.

I was filled with joy as God unfolded the revelation to me. However, I've learned that it's one thing to dream and another thing to cast that vision in front of the people. Our church had grown, but mainly with poor people. Our offerings didn't add up to much.

After seeing the vision, I started casting the vision. And I began with my father. Since he is the founder, I thought he should know first. My father was in Nashville for a preaching engagement, and I caught him just before he left his hotel. I excitedly told him of the hospital, how enormous it was, how perfect it was. My father calmed me down and told me he would come and see it soon. When my father was able to evaluate the site in person, he saw the same things I did. He even added ministries to my list. Together, we saw the reality of the vision. Day and night, the dream consumed us.

Many nights, I drove to the center of the campus, got out of my car, and said, "Dear God, this seems impossible, but please give us this hospital." It was with me every night, the dream of restoring the old building so that thousands of poor, sick, hurting people could learn of the love of Jesus.

COUNTING THE COST

We were determined to buy the building that had a price tag of more than $4 million. At one time the asking price was $16 million. But the years had taken their toll, and even at the reduced price no one was willing to buy the property. For eight years, Hollywood produced movies from the building. Since it was empty, moviemakers could tear it apart, create the sets they wanted, and use the hospital for scenes in some of Hollywood's biggest movies, such as *Ghost* and *Nixon*.

At first, my father and I were a bit intimidated by the cost: so were the church members. Most of them were homeless, on welfare, or from the streets, and we were talking about buying a building for $4 million. It was a tremendous financial risk, but the Assemblies of God, who owned Bethel Temple, were willing to take it. A part of the contract specified that we had to raise the money in eighteen months or our current building would be put up for sale. It was a huge risk. Some people thought we were crazy and criticized us for being irresponsible. But it takes a big dream to make a difference in a big city.

You can't reach Hollywood unless you have a vision that's as big or bigger than Hollywood. You can't reach a gang-infested area unless your dream of changing it is as big as the gangs' desire to destroy it. We accepted the challenge and presented it to the church. The members decided to back us—financially and spiritually—in our efforts to do the impossible.

For eighteen months, my father gave every bit of himself to raise the money. Speaking in church after church with little sleep or rest, flying from one city to another receiving offerings, the man was determined. Many days I thought that he might not be able to make it much longer without rest, but he always reached deep inside his soul and was able to do one more thing, speak one more time, fly to one more city, no matter how hard it was. The dream captured his heart as well as his mind. Everywhere we went we spoke of the dream. We were a team, and we shared every daily miracle on the phone. We rejoiced when money came in. We mourned when it seemed that we wouldn't meet our goal. But we gave it a try.

In life, it's better to have a dream and give it a try than to live in mediocrity. It's better to give the impossible a chance. The worst thing that can happen is that you go back to where you started. When the team is losing by one point, no time is left on the clock, and someone has to shoot two free throws, the winner wants the ball. His philosophy is, "I prefer to risk being called a failure if there's a chance that I can have a shot at glory." We really believed that if God was going to shake the city, we needed to put Him to the test, or better yet He needed to put us to the test, and He did.

Amazing things happened! Financial miracles occurred every time our backs were against the wall. Twenty dollars, fifty dollars, thousands of dollars—it took a little of everything to raise the money. It was done by sweat, tears, and a little blood. All the way to the end, we had to endure, but when it was all said and done, we had the money. We were like the little boy who wants to buy ice cream. He doesn't have much money, so he brings his pennies to pay for it and somehow counts out just enough. We had enough, but that was about it.

When all was said and done, the Dream Center was paid for by faithful people across America who gave because of the dream of restoring a city. And we continue to live by miracles month after month. God always comes through.

Even now, as I'm reliving the miracle of God's provision, it brings me to tears. A twenty-year-old young man, scared of his shadow, with his nearly sixty-year-old father did it! And I had to pastor the church by myself. I made all the decisions. My father promoted the Dream Center, raised money for it, and acted as a spiritual mentor to the staff, but for the most part I was alone. But with God we can do all things.

When the property was declared ours officially, I went to the roof of the main hospital building. I looked out and saw the beautiful skyline of the city of Los Angeles and the thousands of homes surrounding the city. I made a pledge to God that day. Because God was so good to bless us with such a place, to provide so faithfully, we would use the place as a center of hope for every boy or girl who had no mom and dad, every hungry soul, every weary soul, and every person who had a broken dream and needed to dream again. Thus, it was declared the Dream Center.

5

THE WELFARE OF THE PEOPLE

NEHEMIAH 2:10 (KJV) RECORDS, "When Sanballat the Horonite, and Tobiah the servant, the Ammonite, heard of it, it grieved them exceedingly that there was come a man to seek the welfare of the children of Israel." The word *welfare* means "well-being, prosperity, health, or happiness." So it could be said that Nehemiah sought the well-being of the people, the prosperity of the people, the health of the people, or the happiness of the people. My favorite leader in all the Old Testament is Nehemiah. Not just because of his ability to build the wall within fifty-two days with a few people, but because of his heart.

Nehemiah was saddened before the king. He must not have been that way before in the king's presence. The king said, "What's wrong?" Nehemiah responded, "My lord, the city that I love is being destroyed, the gates are burned with fire, and I'm troubled." The king asked, "What do you want?" Nehemiah stated, "Permission to go home and help rebuild the city."

You see, Nehemiah didn't set out to be a great leader. His heart was broken for the hurts of his people. He saw that life could be better for them. He saw that they could be more prosperous, and he wanted to do whatever he could do to make life better for the people he loved. He saw the destruction of the city, he saw the poverty, he saw how the city lost its glory, and his heart was touched. Nehemiah didn't go to be a leader; he went to serve. He didn't go to preach a great sermon; he went to serve. He went to build, to support, to try to make life better for the people. He sought the welfare of the people.

TRUE LEADERSHIP

The greatest leaders are people who never set out to be leaders. True leaders don't elevate themselves. Instead, the people elevate them. Great leaders are like Nehemiah. They become leaders because they learn what leadership is all about, serving the people.

As a twenty-year-old pastor, I couldn't forcefully declare myself a leader. I had to earn the respect of the people. I gained it by serving the people, by getting out into the streets with them. I've earned it every Saturday by going into the neighborhood cleaning the streets, visiting the people, and working with them. Some young men make a mistake in ministry by forcefully proclaiming that they are leaders. In fact, they love the power; they love to have authority and control over people because their egos get a boost. But they fail to realize that the power is not for them; it's for serving others.

True leaders don't want to be leaders, but they are declared leaders because of their love for the people. Just because a person has a title doesn't make him a leader. The title doesn't make the person; the person makes the title.

After we purchased the hospital, my dream was to find a group of people with that same heart. The Dream Center's building required a lot of work on it, and we had a long way to go. In my heart, I felt that it would take five years to get going, but God sent me a team of people whose hearts were for the welfare of the people. He also sent others whose hearts were for personal gain, and to this day, many want to jump on the bandwagon of the Dream Center miracle. But in this business of working in the inner city, it doesn't take long to recognize the true leaders.

HOLLYWOOD MINISTERS

Who are these leaders? They are right in front of pastors. They serve faithfully and love people. They love the pastor by loving all people without partiality. Their goal is not to be seen, but to do, and their character shines as a testimony to all. You can find them in a heartbeat if you look for the right qualities.

Not long after we moved to our new site, a man walked into my office. He was dressed humbly and spoke in one of the sweetest voices I've ever known. He wasn't trying to impress me but wanted to share his vision with me. He didn't have charts, statistics, or a slick sales presentation. He just spoke with simple compassion.

Clayton Golliher told me that for the last seventeen years he had worked on the streets of Hollywood ministering to the runaway and throwaway kids of Hollywood Boulevard. Many nights, he searched through the back alleys of Hollywood and ministered to little boys and girls living in garbage cans. He gave them food, and sometimes he slept beside them to relate to their pain and to identify with the people. He has given his life to a generation of kids who came to Hollywood to seek a dream, only to have that dream turned into a nightmare as they ended up homeless on the cold streets that they once thought were glamorous.

All those years, he walked the streets proclaiming Jesus and rescuing kids. He took them into his house, but he could do only so much. In reality, he didn't have an adequate place to shelter the kids.

Clayton is a modern-day hero, a saint on the streets of Hollywood. You may visit Hollywood Boulevard and see Clayton talking to some kids with spiked hair, ministering to a prostitute, or giving encouragement to a boy who lives in a Dumpster.

After hearing his stories, I knew he was a leader. I knew he belonged on our team, and from that day, he has been on the staff of our church. Every Thursday night he brings a bus full of kids from the street to our services. Some of them haven't showered in a week. Some of them might even be high coming into the service. In one case, a kid brought his pet rat into church, but Clayton sits by them and loves them. Clayton came to Hollywood to seek the welfare of the people.

A Basic Philosophy

Nehemiah became a great leader because the people could tell that his heart was for them. Nehemiah worked with the people, and that made his mission successful. At our church, every person in the community knows what we are about. They might not be Christians, but all of them know the philosophy of our church. We send out trucks that distribute food to tens of thousands of people every week. We hold church services in nearly thirty poor neighborhoods a week, ministering to kids and families, and outreaches go out every day. At one o'clock each day, people gather around the campus and prepare to invade the streets of our city ministering to kids and hungry families. We provide food daily to thousands of homeless men and women living under the bridges of our city.

My father and I seem to spend most of our time identifying needs in the community and meeting those needs. Today, more than two hundred outreach programs are a part of this church. Nearly all of them were started by seeing the needs and then creating ministries to meet those needs.

In our community, crime has dropped dramatically in the last three years. In fact, crime has dropped every year since the Dream Center was established. Homicides alone have dropped 73 percent in the last four years. We can't say that we've stopped someone from pulling a trigger, but we can say that when hundreds of caring people invade a neighborhood with love day after day, week after week, without stopping, the atmosphere of the community changes.

When I first started ministering here, every night was the same: a police helicopter flying over, shootings in the streets, young men lined up with their hands over their heads against a police car. That's all changed now. Sure, from time to time there is trouble, but the atmosphere of love, giving, and serving has changed the spirit in the air.

REAL REVIVAL

In America today, we hear much talk of revival and change in our cities. We think that somehow it's just going to happen or fall out of the sky. Things don't happen that way. There is no shortcut to revival. It takes prayer, and a lot of determined people in the trenches getting the job done day after day. We can have a great move of God in a church service, but we cannot declare it revival unless real change occurs in our world.

To me, real revival comes when the crime rate drops, communities are changed for the better, people in the community flock to the church, and the spirit of the area changes in a positive way.

Revival came in the book of Acts, but there was tremendous dedication in the hearts of the apostles who followed that tremendous filling of the Spirit in the Upper Room. After being filled with the Holy Spirit, the men went everywhere, starting churches and ministries, and they changed the world. They gave of themselves all that they had. That's what it will take to change our cities: a tremendous desire in leaders to give of themselves, to give their lives for the welfare of a community or a city.

"WHAT WILL YOU GIVE TO THE KING?"

I love this story. An older man was walking down the streets of Chicago on a cold winter night. It was Christmas, and he was heading for the local mission, hoping to get something to eat. He got a little meal, and when he was satisfied, he left the chow hall and went back outside to the streets.

All of a sudden, he saw a sign outside the mission that read, "What will you give to the King?" Next to the sign was a garbage can for donations. The homeless man looked at the sign, and he was intrigued, so he reached into his pocket, took out a quarter, and put it in the garbage can.

He walked down the road, and as he did, he couldn't get the words out of his mind, *What will you give to the King?* He turned around and went back to the mission to make another donation. He reached into his pocket, grabbed smaller change, and placed it in the garbage can. After soothing his conscience, he continued to walk. He was quite a distance away, yet he was still haunted by the sign, "What will you give to the King?" He went back, reached into his pocket, but had no more money. He was perplexed. He felt that he *had* to give something, but what more could he give? Suddenly the older man lifted his right foot, then his left, and placed himself in that old garbage can, for he said, "I will give of myself." Can't you picture that sight? I think he understood what it was all about.

If you think that you have nothing to give, if you feel that you have no talent, just give of yourself. Lay down your life for another. Give all of your hopes and dreams to make life better for people, and watch what God will do in your life. You don't have to be highly educated, talented, or charming to do something for God. Just be available.

EVERYONE IS A MINISTER

The secret to our church is that everyone is a minister. Everyone has a desire to help another person. About seventy members stand in line to greet all the people as they come into a service. The goal is to create the atmosphere, "We love you, and we want to lift your spirits." People respond by saying, "I've never felt such joy." The people are trained to seek the welfare of others. We are a team with a common goal. We don't dream alone; we dream together.

No matter how long it takes our pastors, they are the last to leave the service, shaking hands with everyone, praying until the last person leaves. The greatest sermon ever preached is not from the pulpit; it's after the service through interaction with people. It's essential to connect with people. That's another wise lesson I've learned from my father. Many nights, he stood outside the door for two to three hours shaking hands with people. Many nights, he and I together turned the lights off in the church. Ministry is about people!

A teen who attends our church is named Jessica. She grew up in the streets of Los Angeles near the Coliseum. She was raised in the gangs and ran with them for several years. She had been riding our buses for some time and was attending our youth services. One night, she accepted Christ in her life.

Our youth pastor stood up and said, "If anyone wants to give up something, ask God to give you the power to do it right now." She told the youth pastor that she was in a gang and wanted out of it. The pastor told her she could do it, but then she cried and said, "In order to do so, I'm going to have to be beaten out of the gang." She was talking about this process: gang members gather around the person and beat her for nearly a minute. Then after she takes the beating, she is allowed to leave. That's the only way out.

This teenager asked if the youth pastor would stand by her and watch so that things wouldn't get out of hand and everyone would abide by the gang code. The youth pastor tried to talk the gang out of it, but couldn't, so he stood by and watched as Jessica was beaten by the other girls. With blood trickling down her face from cuts, she looked like an angel as she told the girls that she now belonged to Jesus and that she would no longer be in the gang. Some may not understand how a pastor could stand by and watch this happen, but being beaten out of a gang is a fact of life on the streets. If Jessica had not gone through with it, the gang would have stalked her until she eventually left the gang by the only means they would accept—being beaten out. The youth pastor was there to make sure the gang released her.

We live for these people, and we fight for these girls. Every day of my life, thinking of the Jessicas and many others helps me put my life in perspective. When I work in the office, when I counsel, when I preach, I keep them in my mind. Doing that helps me to go on and keep giving.

Multitudes of people give up on their dream because their focus is wrong. Instead of going on because they are committed to people, some give up because they don't see physical results. My father has a saying that I've adopted for my life: "I will never use my people to build my ministry. I will use my ministry to build my people." He is saying, "I will use my ministry to seek the welfare of the people."

A TEACHER'S DREAM

A Christian school for inner-city children operates in the Dream Center. Once a year I'm the substitute teacher, and I need much prayer for that task. For one hour, I have an open discussion with the students about many things. Most of our students—in fact, 75 percent of them—come from single-parent homes. I told the kids in the class that I wanted every one of them to tell me their dreams. One by one, I heard the stories, everything from sports athletes to fashion designers to marine biologists.

I encouraged them to reach their dreams and never to give up in their pursuit. As I was closing the discussion, one young man asked me, "Pastor, what is your dream?" The question threw me off guard. I knew of things I wanted to accomplish and dreams I wanted to bring to reality in the church. However, I wanted to give him the truth of the greatest single longing of my heart. I thought about him, and the answer came easily. Tears welled up in my eyes as I looked at those precious students raised in broken homes. I smiled and said, "My dream is to see that all of your dreams come true."

6

GOD BELIEVES IN YOU
AND SO DO I

AMONG THE MEN in the Bible whom I admire, there is one who was not a prominent leader or an apostle, someone who penned a great book of the Bible, or someone who was a part of the ministry of Jesus Christ. His name was Barnabas.

A WORLD CHANGER

Let me first tell you what he meant to the apostle Paul. The apostle Paul changed the world because he took the gospel to the Western world, to Europe, and from Europe it came to our country. However, Barnabas had a tremendous effect on Saul of Tarsus, later known as Paul.

Saul of Tarsus was a Pharisee, breathing threats against Christian people, threatening to slaughter them. In some cases he oversaw the murder of God's people. He did it because he thought it was right. He was on a mission to destroy Christians.

One day, he was on his way to Damascus to do the same

thing, and on the road he had an amazing vision (Acts 9:1–31 NKJV). He looked up, and a light shone round about him. A voice from heaven said, "Saul, Saul, why are you persecuting Me?" Saul said, "Who are You, Lord?" The Lord responded, "I am Jesus, whom you are persecuting." Saul was persecuting the Lord by persecuting His people.

Something real happened to Saul, and he knew that the Lord had spoken to him. He responded, "Lord, what do You want me to do?" He had just become a follower of Christ, and he already wanted to sign up. He wanted to evangelize ten minutes after being converted.

Saul was saved because of his amazing experience, then baptized and filled with the Holy Spirit. He started to preach in the synagogues. You see, he was a Pharisee and welcomed in the synagogues. He was a big shot. Saul had an open invitation, and he stood up and said something like this: "You know, we study the Old Testament. Let's study Isaiah 53." Then he said, "I just met the person Isaiah 53 was talking about. I saw him on the Damascus road." His preaching irritated the religious leaders who didn't believe in Jesus of Nazareth. They tried to kill Saul and pursued him to take his life.

The main problem was that when Saul arrived in Jerusalem to preach, the Christians there were afraid of him. That shouldn't be surprising. Let's suppose there was a guy who was killing Christians in your community, and all of a sudden he wanted to preach at your church. You'd say, "Hold it right there. You're not going to preach here." They didn't trust Saul. They didn't believe that he was sincere or even a Christian. Now enter my hero Barnabas. Barnabas believed in him. He stood with Saul and said to the people, "You listen to this man."

Barnabas was well respected. People listened to what he had to say, and what he said carried a lot of weight. If Barnabas had not believed in Saul, then we might not know God today or know who God is. Thank God that Barnabas believed in the new convert, and because of that, the gospel was taken to the Western world.

But that's not all! John Mark was a nephew of Barnabas. When the apostle Paul went on his first missionary journey, he took John Mark with him to preach. They went everywhere, preaching in Cyprus, Antioch, Derbe, and Lystra. Then they returned home to report to the church the results of their first journey.

After a season, they were to set out on the second missionary journey, and Barnabas said, "It's time for us to leave. So, Paul, let's take John Mark." Paul said, "No." Paul refused to take John Mark with them. The reason was that in Pamphylia, John Mark turned back and left Paul on the journey. No one knows why John Mark turned back. Maybe he feared the wild beasts, or maybe he was homesick. But he turned back. Paul would not take him again because he felt that John Mark turned on him and became a coward when things got tough.

Barnabas and Paul had a harsh disagreement. Finally Barnabas decided that he would take John Mark, and Paul took Silas with him (Acts 15:36–40). Now I understand why Paul was upset, but Barnabas was right in this situation. Why? Because Barnabas believed in John Mark. Think about it! If it weren't for Barnabas, who believed in Paul, we wouldn't have had the apostle Paul, who has greatly influenced our lives. Also, if it weren't for Barnabas, we wouldn't have had Mark, who wrote the second of the four Gospels. The two men would change the course of Christianity and civilization all because Barnabas had the courage to believe in them.

WE BELIEVE IN THEM

Every successful person owes his success to someone who believed in him. I believe that every young person would turn out right if he was convinced that someone genuinely loved him and believed in him. I often tell young people in our neighborhood that I believe in them. They light up, and sometimes those words allow them to start changing as individuals. Most of the young men and women in our neighborhood are single-parent kids, their dads are alcoholics, many parents are bound by drugs. When we tell them that we believe in them, they might not have heard those words before.

In our neighborhood drug usage and addictive behavior are too common problems. As a pastor, I can never lose hope. I have to believe that every young girl who has had a baby out of wedlock can make it and become pure and live a godly life. I have to believe that the man who comes into our rehab program with a drug addiction can be changed.

The power to believe provides the power to change. I believe that our community is salvageable. I believe that it's not impossible to overcome a drug addiction. I believe that there is one section of the city where people can say, "There is hope in that neighborhood." Without that hope you cannot see great change in lives or a world.

What is hope? It's Moses telling Joshua he believed in him, giving him courage, and motivating him to lead the people. It's Jesus telling the crooked tax collector Matthew to follow Him. It's Jesus telling Zacchaeus hiding up in a tree to come down because He wants to have dinner with him. It's Jesus believing in a group of common fishermen to do an uncommon work.

Mother Teresa touched the world as few people in history have done. However, Mother Teresa was not initially permitted to work with the poor, which was her greatest desire. She taught in a private school for kids from a higher economic background. I read that she used to look out her window and see disabled people on the streets, and it was in her heart to work for them. She pleaded and pleaded for the chance but never got it—until one day, a priest gave her the chance to work with the "poorest of the poor." Mother Teresa went on to do a great work, but before she did that great work, there was a priest who believed in her.

The gospel in itself is the most beautiful story of all of a Savior who believed in the people He loved. He believed in them so much, He laid down His life for them. In the Christian world, we tend to live our lives with a "what have you done for me lately?" mentality. Instead, we should not be concerned about what others do for us. We should believe in others to help them achieve their dreams.

PERSISTENT, CONSISTENT BELIEF

Someone from the church visited Omar every week for nearly three years. He was a nice young man, but he ran with the wrong crowd. Nearly every night, a party or something wild was going on at his house. He was a leader in the neighborhood, and many of the gang members hung out at his house to drink. He was invited several times to our church, but always graciously declined.

Many young men raised in the streets of Los Angeles are tough, but if you really love them, they will respect you. You have to earn that respect, and you do it by being consistent in their lives, showing them week after week that you really do care.

Ken visited Omar week after week and never let up on him. Finally one Sunday, Omar came to church. He didn't give his life to the Lord, but he liked the church, the music, the enthusiasm, and came back several times to visit. I was always concerned for Omar and hoped that one day something would click inside him and he would receive the Lord.

At the end of one service, I saw Omar out in the audience, and I called him up to the stage. He was terrified because he didn't know what I was going to do. I took off my brand-new suit jacket and gave it to him. I told him that it wasn't a magic coat or anything special. I told him I wanted to give it to him to let him know that I believed in him. Every time he looked at that jacket I wanted him to know that I believed in him.

Since that day, Omar has been a stick of dynamite for the Lord. He goes out with me every Saturday and visits people and tells them of the change that has taken place in his life. Often when he tells people where he lives, they are astonished and say, "I didn't think there was hope for anyone in that place." They had seen all of the activity at that house and couldn't believe change had come there. I believe that Omar is going to become a powerful force for God and for good in our community.

Many churches across the country have started to bus in homeless people to church services. One person might get out of line, and the church members might complain and stop picking them up for church because they seem to be distractions. Never give up! If you continue to believe in people, someday something great will happen that will knock even the greatest optimist off his feet.

HOPE FOR THE SEEMINGLY HOPELESS

I have seen too much not to believe that anyone can change. A few years ago a man came to our church who had been bound by drugs for thirty-five years. Billy used to play lead guitar for some of the biggest acts in the music industry. He played for Little Anthony, for example. Drugs pounded Billy's life until he was nearly left for dead. Here is Billy's story in his own words:

I am fifty-one years of age. I have played music most of my life. I was a drug addict for thirty-five years. I lost everything—my self-respect, dignity, and my family. My children were taken away.

When I was at the end of my rope scraping the bottom to look up, I begged Jesus into my life. Jesus entered my life like a bolt of lightning and started a fire in me that cannot be put out.

I have been here, at the Dream Center, for three years now, and I have learned the meaning of true love.

My Jesus has restored my family. My Jesus has given me back my self-respect. My Jesus has given me a reason to live. My Jesus is blessing me and my family beyond measure.

Now, it is my duty and my pleasure to help others. To bring joy into people's lives. To bring hope in Jesus' name.

I now have a ministry called the LAIC Aids Project, and I am the guitar player for the Praise and Worship band.

I also work security at LAIC.

I thank my Jesus for a pastor who knows nothing but love and compassion.

If I had one wish it would be to share the joy, love, and truth which Jesus has given me.

Growing up in a pastor's home, I have met some of the most famous ministers in the world, men of God who've done incredible things. I've also seen some of them fail. Many pastors' kids become disillusioned when they see men of God not live up to the standards they profess. However, I believe in people, and I know that in the heart of man is a desire to do what is good. I choose to see that side of man. You see, God believes in you and so do I.

7

THE CHURCH OF THE NEW MILLENNIUM

USUALLY WHEN PEOPLE talk about the inner city, their attitude is that of hopelessness. The mind-set is something like this: let's drop a bomb on it and start all over. The needs of the inner city seem endless. Growing up, I was spoiled. If I wanted something to eat, I could have it whenever I wanted. That's not the case in the inner city.

Every day a truck from the church distributes food to some of the poorest neighborhoods in the city. Families line up for blocks to get one bag of basic groceries.

I'm from a middle-class home and a white-collar city. I grew up hearing, "This is America. You can be whatever you want to be." I believe in that, but it's not always easy when you come from third-generation welfare recipients or you come from an immigrant family. When you're a poor immigrant, there is little opportunity for you. Many don't have time to learn English. They have to find a job quickly, and when they do, it's a low-paying service job. Their sons and daughters have to be mouthpieces for them because they lack the skills to speak the English language, and the children don't have the chance to socialize like other teenagers. The welfare system doesn't work for them. Only a strong, thriving church is the answer.

INNER-CITY NEEDS

We need thousands of inner-city churches across America that will be open every day to meet the social needs of the people. We need churches that will be centers of activity for communities. Energy, excitement, and hope need to be transmitted into our cities. In LA, many churches have bars on their windows and doors as if to say, "We are afraid of you. Don't come in." Our church doesn't believe that! Our church has no bars, no barriers, nothing to exclude the people we are trying to reach.

Active ministry is very important in the community for many reasons. The first is that you are helping people. The second is that being active and visible creates positive energy in the neighborhood. The Dream Center has changed the course of our community. When we first started ministering, the streets were dark and cold. Now there is a warmth obvious to anyone who has been here a while. It's a basic idea. When hundreds of people hit the streets, give food, and clean the streets every day, there is going to be positive change.

Churches that are built on active ministry will stand the test of time when churches that are built on trends come and go. That's why we teach principle at our church because principle will go on when trends die. For years, we Americans have believed the crazy notion that it's the government's job to be involved with social programs and it's the church's job to win souls. We separate serving others from saving souls. However, to believe that is to go against the teachings of Jesus and the example of Jesus. Everything that we do, helping in a social way, promotes the winning of souls.

ADOPT-A-BLOCK

One program in our church has revolutionized our ministry. It is called Adopt-a-Block. Every church member is encouraged to be a part of this ministry. In fact, all of our residents and our pastoral staff participate on Saturdays. I tell my pastoral staff that they all need to be there every week because I want them to have a heart for individuals and to be in touch with what is going on in our community. Many pastors know only preaching, doing office work, and dealing with church administration. They fail to realize the great joy of going out to the neighborhoods and talking with people one on one, serving the people, and pouring their hearts out for a community. Every Saturday for three hours I minister on the block I've adopted, and it has changed my life and perspective of ministry. If my heart is not connected to my city, I can't be the man God has called me to be.

The Adopt-a-Block program was started one Saturday when I walked around the neighborhood and saw how the different religions ministered to people. I watched the Jehovah's Witnesses, the Mormons, and others. I noticed that many people opened their doors and listened, but they didn't respond. They felt that they were obliged to listen, but they seemed to be thinking, *I wish I hadn't opened the door*.

The representatives of those religions appeared to want to spread their message, but they didn't seem to convey an equally sincere feeling of love to the people. I believe in street ministry. I believe in door-to-door soul winning. I am an old-fashioned, "you must be born again" kind of guy. Don't be mistaken. I want people to come to Jesus Christ, but I want something more than that. I want to win them, train them, see them become faithful members of the church, active in ministry, and I want to follow them years down the road and become a part of their lives.

Those delivering the message seemed to fail to connect with the people on a personal level. I wanted to start a program that would shake the community and add multitudes to the house of God. My dream was to look out every Sunday morning and see masses of people walking to church from the local community.

The Lord gave me the plan. Every Saturday we adopt thirty blocks in our neighborhood. Four people become pastors of that block, and they are responsible to take care of it. For the first couple of months we do nothing but care for the needs of the people. We go to the door and say, "We are your neighborhood servants assigned to this block, and we are here to serve you. What can we do to help?"

For the first few weeks, we build relationships with people, serve them, and give toys or candy to the kids. For years afterward, we minister on the same block to the same people, and we become a part of their lives. We pastor that block for a lifetime. Visitors who accompany us comment, "I can't believe the kind of relationships your church has built." I tell them it's simple because we know the people and we've made it a point to be in their lives.

After we visit all of the people, we walk throughout the block and pick up the garbage. We place it on a flatbed truck that drives around and collects the trash for all thirty blocks. It's an incredible sight: hundreds of people spend three hours every Saturday serving hurting people. We may mow the lawns, paint houses, give away groceries, have contests between the blocks with the kids, hand out hamburgers, or throw block parties. We've probably followed through on one hundred other ideas. All of our efforts are made to connect with people.

As a result, my dream has come true. Every Sunday morning people from the community walk to the church because a group of people are faithful every week in serving others.

I get great joy out of speaking at conferences or being on television. But it does not compare to the joy I receive every Saturday when I look at the faces of those little children who wait by the door for us. I put on casual clothes, get my bag of candy and sack of toys, and feel like Santa Claus spreading joy and showing people that Christians really do love. It's a good feeling to know that we know the names of the families on our block. I don't know of a program that has added more people to the local church than this one. The secret of ministry is building relationships and paying the price week after week to make a difference in a community.

Permission to Dream

The church of the new millennium will have to be a permission-giving church where people are allowed to start new and unique ministries. You need to cast a vision for the change you want to make in your city, tell people that you want them to be a part of the vision, and then let them dream. Not all might be preachers or teachers or musicians, but many will astonish you with what they can do if you will release them.

My father preaches a sermon entitled "There's a Miracle in Your House." The basis of the sermon is that everything you need to build a great church is already in front of you; you just have to find it. I believe that! And our church lives by that.

A young woman, nineteen years of age, stopped by my office one day, and we talked about ministry. She had been serving faithfully at our church and was helping in the outreach ministries. She had a dream of feeding thousands of people every day throughout the city of Los Angeles. The first thing that came to my mind was, *How are you going to do it?* However, I listened, and at the end of our conversation, I saw the same determination in this 115-pound young woman that I had when I started in the ministry at age seventeen. I had no direction. I told her that I could give her a beat-up truck and she could do what she felt led to do.

Well, she took my challenge and started a new ministry called Acts 29. She lifted heavy boxes, made phone contacts to get all of the food, and spent day after day working to the bone to see it become a reality. She made connections with the United States Department of Agriculture, grocery stores, and community organizations.

After one year, she is now taking that truck to some of the poorest neighborhoods and serving ten thousand people a week, and that doesn't include all the other feeding programs in the church. She has a full-time staff of three people who go out five days a week and hold outdoor services while distributing food. To be honest, I was impressed by the young woman's heart for the poor, and she wasn't bad looking either (more to be said of that in the final chapter).

CONNECT WITH THE PEOPLE

The day is coming when pastors won't preach just to a congregation but will preach to members who in turn will act as ministers by carrying out the message of God's love on a daily basis. Some of our sanctuaries need to be open during the week for practical programs that will connect with people. Every Tuesday and Friday I teach a wrestling class for kids in our community in the same sanctuary where we have church.

We are constantly looking for needs and fulfilling them. For example, we started a free medical clinic. Doctors are lined up and ready to help, and we believe that hundreds of people will seek treatment on a weekly basis. In many cases, our facility is the only one that can help them because of their financial lack. Also, we are starting a home for unwed pregnant women because we've identified a big problem with teenage pregnancy.

Where do you find these needs? You don't have to look far. Just look anywhere. When I mention all of these needs to pastors or workers—bringing homeless people, runaway kids, drug addicts, and gang members into the church—some of them respond, "What will that do to families in the church? How in the world will they accept it?" Believe it or not, our church has been able to cross all barriers of church growth. All my life I've been told that it's nearly impossible to bring all of these different kinds of people together. You have either an upper-class church or a lower-class church. We believe that we ought to have an every-class church. It was said of the church of the book of Acts, "They had all things in common" (4:32 NKJV). That is what a New Testament church is all about. The poorest of the poor, middle-class families who drive from hours away, and celebrities such as Dyan Cannon and Lou Rawls—all attend our church. Most of the middle-class families attend because of what we do for poor and hurting people. A group of influential people out there want to be part of a church that's making a practical, tangible change in the streets.

THE CHURCH'S RESPONSE TO UNCERTAINTY

There is much uncertainty about the future: fear of the new millennium, fear of Y2K. Many people are storing food, buying ranches, and thinking about getting away from it all. There is no greater time for the church to make a difference than now. I don't know what will happen with the year 2000, but I do know one thing. We will be ready, we will be here at the old hospital, and if anything drastic takes place, the old lighthouse will be on. We will do what we've always done—meet needs, care for people, love the poor, and make sacrifices for people in need.

I challenge any pastor reading this book to motivate your people to get out into the streets and make a difference. Set the example, turn your people loose to do ministry, and cast the vision of a changed community, town, or city to your people. In the new millennium, the church will face many challenges, but if every church became a healing center in its community, we could set in motion a brand-new way of life, a brand-new way of thinking, a fresh new approach to ministry. I believe that the world would see the church in a different way. There is no better time than now to raise up beacons of light in our communities because we have a fresh start with a brand-new millennium. What an opportunity to demonstrate true love in action!

8

WHY DO GOOD?

I'VE TOLD YOU beautiful stories of lives that have been changed in the inner city, but doing what we do isn't always pretty.

One day, after the service was over and people were filtering out of the building, a man approached me. He looked familiar, but I couldn't recall who he was. His hair was gray, and he was very thin. He came closer, and I finally recognized him. We had been picking up this man for more than a year on the buses, and he had always been very friendly but quiet. He had a concerned look on his face as he said, "I know how your church can get a lot of attention."

I asked, "How?"

He then said in a threatening tone, "I'm going to kill you and then kill myself." He pulled out a gun and repeated, "I'm going to kill you."

Despite my fear, I looked him in the eye and stated calmly, "Sir, you can kill me. I know exactly where I am going to go, but I'm concerned for you and where you're going to spend eternity."

He pushed me against the wall and told me to beware

before he ran from the building. In the next month of March, he was going to kill me on a Sunday. He said, "See if your God can save you."

THE POWER OF DESPAIR, THE POWER OF GOD

That month I've never walked closer to the Lord. Somehow week after week the man sneaked into church and stalked me. Our security people wanted to take him out as soon as he came in, but something inside me said to let him come. During my sermons, I looked out at the audience, and there he was, making gestures as if he were going to do some harm. It was hard to preach and keep my mind on my sermon, but I did it anyway.

After every service, he threatened me: "Next week is the week." I believed him. He was angry because he was dying of AIDS and felt that nobody cared for him. He wanted to draw attention to his plight, and by killing both of us, he would show the world how frustrated he really was. He was going to die anyway, so what did he have to lose?

I'm not that brave, but something told me to allow him to come to church and have some people keep a close eye on him. I became extra cautious in all that I did.

After a Saturday night service, I felt a tap on my shoulder. I turned around, and there he was standing right in front of me. He asked me if I would like to step outside. At that moment two thoughts ran through my mind.

First, I should not go outside because he was going to kill me. Second, if I backed down and showed weakness, he might not respect me as a pastor. I decided to go outside and talk with him.

We walked down an alley just behind the church, and we talked. The man started to cry uncontrollably. He told me again that he was dying of AIDS and that he was ashamed of the life he had led. As he told me the story, I could see all of his defenses unravel, and he exposed his heart to me. He said, "Every time I watch you preach as a young man, I think of all that I could have become. I love you and respect you, and I could never do you any harm, but at the same time I despise you."

We talked for a while, and he told me of all the regrets in his life and his feelings for me of admiration and jealousy that led to hatred. But the Lord touched his heart, and he cried on my shoulder for what seemed like an eternity. I led him in a prayer, and he accepted Jesus into his life. The next day, he stood up and testified to the church of what he had been planning to do and how the Lord touched his life. Everyone in the church was shocked.

The next day I took him out to lunch by myself and bought him a ticket for the next train to San Francisco where he could be treated for his condition. The bond between us was strong, and after he arrived in San Francisco, he called me a couple of times to let me know he was fine. What a miracle!

GODLY INCENTIVES TO DO GOOD

During the time of testing, the questions came to my mind, *Why do good? Why help this man? Why continue to reach out to him when he desires only to do harm to me?* Some people don't appreciate what you are trying to do for them. Sometimes the people you help the most are the very ones who will walk all over you and take advantage of you the moment they have the chance. So why do good?

In the Bible, God uses many incentives to urge us to do good. First, God uses the fear of punishment. He shows us that if we do evil, the consequences are death and eternity in hell. This fear of punishment brings us closer to Him and is an incentive to do good. But that's not the greatest reason to do good.

Second, God uses rewards. A good example appears in Matthew 11:28 (KJV), "Come unto me, all ye that labor and are heavy laden, and I will give you rest." The incentive of rest entices us to want to do good. Also, there is the incentive of eternal life in heaven for doing good. But there's a better reason for doing good than that.

The greatest reward of all, the one that exceeds all others, is the reward of no reward. It's the peace of knowing that you did what was right. It's the reward of standing alone by yourself for something you know to be right and not wavering. When all the other kids in school are taking drugs at a party, you stand alone and live a pure life. It's the feeling you get when you go to bed at night after a day of making hard decisions; things didn't go your way, but you made your decisions based upon principle, and doing right brings you great peace. When you get to the place in your life that you do what is right for no other reason than because it's right, you have found joy. Doing good carries with it its own rewards.

Bobby Knight is a great basketball coach. Although I don't approve of all his methods, I came to like him when I became familiar with some of his philosophy. There are times when his team wins games and he is not happy, but there are other times when his team loses and he feels at perfect peace. His point: place more attention on effort than on results. Too many people are concerned about achieving, but they never find happiness because they are looking for the result of success to bring joy.

The Dream Center has become successful, but it's not the overall big project that brings me joy. It's knowing that individual lives are being changed for the better.

Praise doesn't bring joy. Awards or acknowledgment doesn't help us find the meaning of life. When we do good because it's right and we want to help people become better, we have found the secret of life. If I never received an award or word of encouragement, I would be happy because my reward is knowing that we ministered to people today and every day.

THE MOTIVATION TO HELP

In the inner city we don't work for reward or praise. In general, needy people don't know how to say, "Thank you." They don't know gratitude. It's not that they don't appreciate what we do. They just don't know how to express it.

Five hundred residents live in the church's facilities on a daily basis. It takes me a long time to walk from my office to my car because many people want to talk to me about their problems. I have to protect myself against becoming hard in spirit. The city is tough, people are hard, and I don't want to conform to this attitude. My desire is to keep my heart soft before people and still cry when I hear the same stories of tragedy. I have to keep my heart prepared at all times. It goes back to motivation. What is my motivation, and why do I do what I do?

I learned this lesson early in my life. My father is one of the most successful church builders of all time; he is a legend in church growth. It's not easy following in his footsteps for many reasons, but it's primarily because people expect great things from me. Whatever I do is not a big deal. If my father weren't a successful pastor and I started the Dream Center, it would be a miracle that an unknown person did something deemed impossible. But people expect me to achieve and accomplish great things because of who I am.

My reason for being a pastor has nothing to do with trying to match my father's accomplishments. God will decide what size church or how much influence He wants me to have. My job is to do good, heal the hurts of the people, be an example in this city, work as hard as I can, and give it my best. If I do good because God said to do it, no reward can compare with being obedient and seeing the effect of my obedience on the lives I touch.

What am I to be? I don't know. But I do know that I don't have to become something great. All I have to do is to focus on being the best servant I can be to this generation. If I find joy in that, I have found happiness.

During our Adopt-a-Block time one Saturday, we were cleaning a street, and a man told me, "You are a pastor. You shouldn't be out here cleaning. These people don't appreciate things, and they are going to mess up the streets, and you're going to have the same problem next week." I replied, "Then we'll be back out the next week." "Why do you do what you do?" he asked. I put down my broom and garbage can and said, "We do it because we love you, and that's the only reason." The man was moved and walked away pondering what I said.

It was hard for him to believe that a group of people simply cared. Why do good anyhow? Because of the peace that settles in your heart, the peace of doing what is right, no matter what.

9

THE BEST LOCATION FOR A CHURCH

I AM NO DIFFERENT from any other pastor. I want the same things most pastors want. Our place of worship isn't the most beautiful place of worship. It's an old gymnasium that has been renovated into a sanctuary. I'm sorry if I've shaken your faith, but our sanctuary is not the architectural envy of modern churches.

Without a doubt, a theater in the suburbs would be nice to have or rent, maybe in Pasadena or Hollywood or Beverly Hills, with a lot of land off a main road. This fantasy has crossed my mind more than once about where I would like to have my church. However, I have noticed that when people leave the downtown area where the poor people live and go to the suburbs to build new churches, the old buildings become grave markers, and the locations become mausoleums. All across America—Miami, New York City, Chicago, Atlanta—buildings of once-thriving ministries have been left behind as monuments of the past.

A Reverse Movement

When these churches moved out of the cities, empty buildings remained in the heart of hurting neighborhoods. But in making a mass exodus from the inner city, many of these churches have died. The dreams of a better life in suburbia have turned into nightmares. The truth is, the beautiful building in suburbia that they felt would be the fulfillment of their dreams and the beginning of a new era became the destruction of their dreams. In our denomination there are fewer than ten English-speaking churches in the city of Los Angeles, the second biggest city in America.

For years, there has been a mass departure from the American inner city. Many of these churches move out to "yuppie communities" and adapt their ministry to that culture, leaving the inner city behind.

Two simultaneous—but opposite—moves are happening. One is the major flight from inner-city areas to so-called greener pastures in suburban areas to plant churches. Another is the movement back to the inner cities.

All over the nation there is a new fire, a new determination, to come back to the cities. Deserted buildings are being converted into centers of hope. A new generation of warriors is buying old strip joints, flophouses, abandoned bars, porno shops, and old churches and using them to win the lost. As a result, this group is building bigger churches, soul-winning churches, than others.

After I moved to Los Angeles, I heard this story many times: "You can't build a church in downtown Los Angeles. There is no money, no future. The secret is to be on the outskirts of the city in Orange County." Nearly every adviser told me that.

Did I think about starting the church in the suburbs? Oh, yes! We explored all of our options, but one day a Scripture came to my mind: "I will also leave in the midst of thee an afflicted and poor people, and they shall trust in the name of the LORD" (Zeph. 3:12 KJV). Where is the best place for a church? In the midst of an afflicted and poor people. I knew we had to build a church in the heart of the city.

Throughout history, the best days of the greatest churches—Spurgeon's tabernacle and others—occurred when they were in the middle of an afflicted and poor people. For five years, we've been in the heart of the city, and we will fight to keep this church in the city. The answer is not to move to suburbia. The answer is to stay where you are and accept a burden for afflicted and poor people.

IN THE MIDST OF THEM

After five years, men from the mission still come to church every Sunday, the runaways are still welcome, we still bus kids from the projects, and multitudes of people who finance the work from middle-class homes still come faithfully. As far as I'm concerned, the Los Angeles International Church will stay in the midst of an afflicted and poor people, and we will reach out to them. You say, "What about the upper class?" They are welcome too. But they are no more welcome than anyone else.

Where are some of the great churches being born? In Beverly Hills? In Colorado Springs? In Palm Beach, Florida? No! In downtown areas. Your church will be successful as long as you continue to reach out to the disabled, sick, and poor people.

People will ask, "Who will pay for all of these services for poor people and all of these buses picking people up?" God. The book of Proverbs is full of promises of provision for those who help poor people:

> He who despises his neighbor sins;
> But he who has mercy on the poor, happy is he.
> (Prov. 14:21 NKJV)
> He who has pity on the poor lends to the LORD,
> And He will pay back what he has given.
> (Prov. 19:17 NKJV)
> He who has a generous eye will be blessed,
> For he gives of his bread to the poor. (Prov. 22:9 NKJV)

Not long ago an influential man showed me a design of what he wanted to help us build. He said, "We can't build this ministry on the poor." He told me he had a lot of money, and we had to build it his way or he wasn't going to help us. The plan of the building was beautiful. I'm talking about millions and millions of dollars for the building.

I told him that wasn't the way we were going to build this church. He said, "Then men like me won't help you and bring in the people with the money." I said, "Okay, but we are not going to forget the hurting." He said, "Then this place won't make it." When someone says that I can't make it, I become more determined to make it. The man left the church and refused to support us.

YOUR BEST SUPPORT

Ladies and gentlemen, you have to believe in your dream because God in heaven supports you and His influence is far greater than the influence of men. As Christians, we should never seek to fight or live in confrontation, but you have to be willing to stand for what you believe in. You need to stand by the vision God has given you and keep it in focus and not let yourself be distracted by the opinions of others.

I've been told more than once that this place would fall apart, but if I took them on a tour today, they would see a debt-free building and a ministry operating on several million dollars a year. They would see a Christian school, two hundred ministries, rehab programs, a church reaching thousands, and thirty thousand people being fed each week in the community.

Why do I want to show the doubters a debt-free building? Because I want to show them how my God loves these poor and afflicted people. It has nothing to do with me. It's all about the love of my Father for His people. I'm so glad that the work of God is not in the hands of a few people with a few dollars. I want to thank God that His work doesn't depend upon those who never win souls, never get on a bus route, never bring anyone to church. The Dream Center is debt free because God finances those who love poor families. We are standing on the promises of almighty God.

A Poor Ghetto Town

Let me take you to Nazareth, a poor ghetto town. Our Lord did not choose to put the Savior in Jerusalem, the center of Judaism. He did not choose to put the Savior in Capernaum. He did not choose to put the Savior in the little town of Bethlehem. He put the Savior in a little town called Nazareth.

Jesus as a young preacher stood in the synagogue to give His first sermon. He quoted Isaiah 61:1 (NKJV):

> The Spirit of the Lord GOD is upon Me,
> Because the LORD has anointed Me
> To preach good tidings to the poor;

He has sent Me to heal the brokenhearted,
To proclaim liberty to the captives,
And the opening of the prison to those who are bound.

Jesus came for five groups of people. First, He came to preach the gospel to the poor. Second, to heal the brokenhearted. Third, to preach the gospel to the captives. Fourth, to recover sight for the blind. And fifth, to set at liberty those who are bruised. That's what the Savior was talking about. Failure to be interested in the poor is failure to become like Jesus.

What a wonderful day in which we live! Never in my life have I seen such a hunger in God's people to minister to hurting people. Other Dream Centers are being established in major cities in America—San Francisco, Seattle, and Columbus, among others—and in foreign countries by people who have come to the Dream Center and caught the vision. We must reclaim our cities for God.

INNER-CITY INFLUENCE

Another factor is affecting our country. The culture of America begins in the inner city. Music trends start in the inner city. Fashion is defined by what kids wear in the inner city. Major companies go to the inner city to find out what's hot and what's not.

Inner-city culture influences music trends in the church. Much of worship in the suburbs has the same flare as that in the inner city. The inner city affects the future of American cities and the world.

It's the latter part of 1999, and I think we'll continue to pick up those little kids with our buses, the homeless will still be invited, the mission men will still be welcome, and God will continue to finance us. The gospel will still be preached, and the church downtown will still be here. The gates of hell shall not prevail against it. We're doing what Jesus did, and we'll stay in the midst of an afflicted and poor people.

Where is the greatest location for a church? Wherever there is the biggest need.

A young woman in the neighborhood spoke to me about how much she loved the ministry and how it had changed her life. Then a look of fear came over her eyes as she said, "Please never leave our area. I don't know what we would do without this church." The young woman hasn't had one consistent element in her life. She has lived a broken life with an unstable family.

My heart was blessed to know that the church was the one good thing in her life she could hold on to. I said, "Do you see all of this work being done on the building and all the money being spent? All of this is for you. We have so much work to be done. We have a big dream for this city, and we are not going anywhere." Her face lit up because she knew that we were here to stay. We need a sincere commitment to our cities once again from people who will drive the stakes in the ground and say, "I think we'll stay here for a while."

10

LOST, DISCARDED, AND ABANDONED

AT TWO O'CLOCK in the morning you can hear the sounds of ministry vehicles getting started as people are gathered in the center of our campus ready to do the work of God. That's right. Evangelism at 2:00 A.M. every Saturday. An army of young people from Hope for Homeless Youth invades the streets of Hollywood with the goal of rescuing teenagers. Teenage boys and girls in prostitution. Kids looking like old men and women because drugs have destroyed their bodies. They are everywhere in Hollywood, these "children of the night."

They arrive all hours of the night at the bus station in Hollywood, some chasing a dream, and some just running away. It is said that if you don't rescue these kids in the first couple of weeks, the pimps will get them, and they will start selling their bodies. Young minds are very impressionable, and these people are forced to do just about anything. Before long, the behavior becomes a way of life for them. The glamorous appeal of the city soon becomes ugly.

In the streets of Hollywood, the young people picked up a beautiful sixteen-year-old. She was a prostitute who had become pregnant. She had the baby and decided to keep it and raise it. She loved the child and cared for it to the best of her ability. One day, her pimp was angry with her because the baby was getting too much attention and she wasn't making any money. He walked in with a gun, put it to the child's head, and pulled the trigger, killing the child. Then he took a hot curling iron and did something so terrible to the mother that she can never have more children. We took her in, and today she is saved, serving God and building a brand-new life away from the pain of where she used to be.

VANISHED GLAMOUR

This kind of story is familiar to me now. These kids are trapped in a world of drug abuse and other nightmares. They do anything to survive. In just a few short weeks their lives can change dramatically and spiral down to a horrible conclusion. These kids live in abandoned buildings, garbage cans, train stations, and dark alleys. Their Hollywood dream vanishes within days.

The Dream Center ministers to this need. In the streets all of the crazy activity happens in the early morning hours. Our youth team hits the streets every week and builds trust with these kids. Some nights they take food to a run-down building where the kids live. Then our workers take sleeping bags and sleep right next to these kids, an act that bonds them together. They can't believe that a group of Christians would sleep in that old building. In one corner, someone will be getting high on a drug. In another corner, someone will be practicing witchcraft. The goal is to provide a spark of hope in their lives.

I've learned that anyone can change. It takes one moment in their lives to trigger that powerful force in them that says, "I can make it, and I can become something greater than this." That's why it pays to be faithful. We never know when that day will come and our love or something we say will be the fuel that will give them the courage to want to change. For some people, that change happens immediately when they feel the love coming from us. For others, it takes years to break through, but one day it will click.

I believe that the heart of man can be awakened, and a powerful counterforce can come against the despair that has prevailed for too long. I believe in feeding programs; however, I believe more in building friendships and long-term relationships because they will produce the change. The food opens the door, and the power of God changes the life.

Not only does Hope for Homeless Youth minister to kids living in abandoned houses, it also ministers to the prostitutes. The young women of the ministry have a wonderful approach to these girls. They treat them with love and respect. When they give the prostitutes roses to let them know that they love them, many of these young prostitutes start to cry. Everyone deserves to be treated with dignity. Homeless people ought to receive a proper handshake and a look in the eye. Likewise, prostitutes ought to feel that we are honoring their dignity. These girls learn that we would lay down our lives for them.

"LOOK EVERYONE IN THE EYE"

John F. Kennedy was setting out for a big political function one day that thousands would attend. He was to meet many people. His wife said something wise: "Honey, there are going to be thousands of people here today, but as you go through the crowd, walk slowly and look everyone in the eye." What great advice! To walk slowly through the crowd and look deep into the eyes of people.

In our society we are taught to walk by people without looking them in the eye. When I was in New York City, I couldn't believe the way people looked straight ahead and walked down the street. On the subways they avoided eye contact with other individuals. When we talk to people, we must make them feel as if we are honoring their dignity. That is what we try to do with the kids on the streets of Hollywood.

Before an evening service, I was introduced to one of these prostitutes, and I told her how excited I was that she was at church. Then another person came by and expressed excitement. Everyone greeted her warmly. She looked at me with astonishment and said, "I don't get it. Why is everyone so nice to me?" She knew only abuse and harsh behavior, and she couldn't believe that someone was happy to see her there.

For many of these girls, we provide shelter, counseling, mentoring, and job training. We help them get back into the flow of society. Some kids don't want to enter the program, but they come on the bus every Thursday and attend our services. They sit on the front row, and nearly all of them are saved when the invitation is given. They are simply looking for someone to love them.

One of our newest ministries reaches out to the pimps. Team leaders march up and down the streets looking for pimps, and they share the gospel with these men. Many of them have come to Christ and changed their way of life.

No one is off-limits on the streets. Our team acts as a search-and-rescue team that owns the streets. The police department has acknowledged that Hollywood Boulevard has been cleaned up from prostitution because of the faithful workers of Hope for Homeless Youth.

The ministry has had a profound impact, and much of the evil activity has been limited over the years. We don't accept the fact that the streets belong to the devil. We claim the streets and believe all of the kids on those streets can be saved. The young people of the ministry are tenacious in their desire to see lives changed.

On Hollywood Boulevard there is the famous Mann's Chinese Theatre, where all of the big Hollywood premieres are shown. One night the line was very long outside the theater. The movie was sold out. As people were waiting to go in, our team walked down the street with a casket as if there were a funeral procession. The sight aroused people's curiosity.

In front of the theater they stopped and opened the casket, and inside were pictures of young people who had died. One by one, they told the stories of how sin destroyed the young lives.

Hope for Homeless Youth ministers to many kids living on beaches. A hot spot is Venice Beach. Thousands of people gather throughout the week and walk up and down the crowded beach. It's the wackiest place on earth. Fortune-tellers, palm readers, a man who calls himself "the world's greatest drunk," New Age prophets, people who think they are God, Muslims telling listeners they are going to hell—you name it, it's going on.

Our team members go to this free-flowing place to tell the story of Jesus in front of thousands of people. One day, they needed someone to play Jesus, and they recruited a young man and told him to put on a robe and play Jesus. He didn't really want to do it. The team didn't know it, but he had been involved in witchcraft and had been a satanic priest. As the story was told, when Jesus was being beaten, the man was so moved, he started to cry. And when the invitation was given, he gave his heart to Christ.

The team took him back to the Dream Center, where he studied to be a preacher.

I could tell you story after story of young lives being rescued out of darkness. In your city, there are young people who are alone and scared and have lost hope. In your church, as an individual, find a way to reach out to these young people. Let's minister to the kids who come to our churches and youth groups, and let's rescue these kids who are perishing, headed for the grave.

Teen Reach

In addition to Hope for Homeless Youth, we have a program called Teen Reach. It's a home for some of the toughest kids in the city. The parents give us permission, and for one year we disciple these troubled kids. However, many times, with the parents' approval, we have to go on what are called search-and-rescue missions. Teen Reach staff go to parties, blend in with the crowd, find the kids, and take them into a separate room to tell them about Jesus. Again, they do all of this with the parents' approval. Later, they take them into the home and teach the kids how to be godly. I have never seen a group of kids more sold out to God. They pray for two hours every morning, and when they pray, the entire church shakes.

One young man's parents brought him to our Teen Reach program. He had a drug problem and had been running with gangs for some time. Within minutes he ran away from the Dream Center. Our search-and-rescue team spotted him down the street and chased him throughout the neighborhood, jumping over fences. One man was even bitten by a dog, but eventually they tracked him down and brought him back. They took him directly into the church service, which was already in progress. The kid didn't want to be there, but at the end of the service a woman told him that he needed to come to God. The kid raised his hand to show that he wanted to accept Jesus, and when he did, thirty other Teen Reach kids surrounded him and started to pray for him for nearly an hour. Then almost the entire church started praying for him, and the kid was saved. Now he is one of the leaders in the program.

Young people are in big need. Growing up, they are surrounded by sin, drug use, and garbage on television, in movies, and on the Internet. Early in life they know much more than any young person should. As a result, we have a broken society, and thousands of broken children live with rage, every sort of perversion, and a devastating loss of hope.

We used to think that violence was an inner-city problem, but we are finding out that the same problem exists in the suburbs. Our young people look for something to live for. They need a cause. They are willing to lay down their lives for anything. They can have all the money in the world, but if they lack a dream, something to live for, their lives will not be fulfilled.

In youth conferences all over America we are teaching our kids the message of abstinence: don't have premarital sex, don't use drugs, and don't drink. Other things need to be taught as well. We need to teach our young people to have a vision. Young people are enticed by the glamour and promises of this world. We need to instill in them to be dreamers at a young age, but in a God-given way.

I read some statistics about the world versus the church in the area of morality. In nearly every area regarding morality, the church was very close to the world. That seems to answer the question about why young people in the church are nearly the same as nonchurched kids in regard to promiscuity and some other issues. Then the Scripture came to mind: "Where there is no revelation [or vision], the people cast off restraint" (Prov. 29:18 NKJV). A vision restrains someone.

If young people have dreams, they won't be in the backseats of cars on Friday night doing what they shouldn't be doing. They realize that living that way is not going to help them reach their dreams. Their dreams are more important than sexual flings. Their dreams keep them within the bounds of what is right and wrong because they don't want to do anything that will hinder the dreams God has given them.

While I was writing this book, I received word that a young man in our streets was shot execution style seven times—four times in the head, three times in the back. A rival gang member ended his life a few blocks away from the church. Why would a young man do that? He had no dream. He had nothing to live for, no thoughts of being a pastor, a doctor, or an honest man. Because he had no dream, he had no restraint and valued nothing. As a result, life meant nothing to him.

Most of the kids we rehabilitate spend one year under close supervision as they are educated here and learn important spiritual lessons. No matter where they come from, when they leave this place, they have a vision and can tell you where they are going or what their dreams are.

Parents, you can give your kid a new car for his sixteenth birthday or the finest labels of the newest clothing line, but if you don't give him a vision, if you don't instill in him the will to believe that he can make a difference in this world, your child can fall away from God. My father always taught me that the vision of serving God is greater than any vision this world has to offer. I believed him, and to this day, I'm compelled to carry that vision.

Let's not forget the children of the night, the ones who have no one to love them, the ones who have already given up on life. Let's love them and encourage them to get back on their feet and dream.

11

DETERMINED TO WIN!

KEVIN BROWN IS the ace pitcher for the Los Angeles Dodgers. I really didn't know much about him until he signed a contract to play with the Dodgers. Our church is only one mile from Dodger Stadium so whenever he is pitching, I want to be at the stadium watching him. He has a tremendous desire to win. He hates to lose!

One night I was watching a game on television, and I noticed that before every pitch he looked as if he were in a trance. He was so focused that he seemed to be in another world. There were tens of thousands of people in that stadium, but he didn't know that they existed because he was focused on his task.

Whenever I need to get motivated, I watch Kevin pitch, and it puts a fire in me. When the inning is over, he goes back to the dugout, sits there, and won't talk to one person on his team for the next three hours. He won't laugh. He won't talk to the coaches. Everyone leaves him alone. He sits there with a determined look and blocks out all other distractions but the game.

His focus is unlike anything I've ever experienced. Some

regard him as a crazy man, but I understand what he is doing. He is taking his job very seriously, and he wants to be successful at it. With such a fierce desire to win, he has become one of the great pitchers of baseball today.

A KEVIN BROWN MENTALITY

I've always believed that Christians should be the most competitive people in the world. We need a Kevin Brown mentality. Every morning, we need to realize that we are working for God and every day counts in the course of eternity.

Every morning, I pump myself up. It's a little mental exercise that prepares me for a big day. I put myself in focus for every task of the day, and I am determined to be at my best, no matter what circumstances come my way.

I've learned in ministry that half the battle is showing up. If you want God to move, the first thing you have to do is to show up. Many people can't even do that! Pastors all over America go to a city, start a church, things don't go well, the battles start to rage, the church doesn't grow, and all of a sudden, they quit and move on. If every pastor stayed in the battle over the years, nearly everyone would be saved in this country. Instead, adverse circumstances occur, failures come, the vision is delayed, and they give up.

This competitive nature needs to be in the hearts of all of us who want to change the cities. We cannot accept losing. The winners of life anticipate the day and expect good things to happen in their favor. Failures get exactly what they expect. My father says, "The very thing you fear is the thing that comes upon you." We need to be confident in the vision that God has given us and believe that the vision is from God and treat it with the care and diligence that it deserves.

Everyone wants to quit at times, and some do quit. But others think about it only for a passing moment. Every time I evaluate the church's financial needs, I am tempted to quit, but I always get back into the game.

We take failure too personally. Instead, we ought to get up after failure and realize that with each day comes a change of tide, and that tide will eventually work back in our favor.

Many of us are afraid to compete. We don't like to be called losers, so we run from big dreams and big goals. Success is not built upon what we achieve, it's built upon effort.

God is not going to judge us on how big a church we built, but He will judge us on the effort we gave in the trenches day after day. When we stand before God, He will say, "Well done, My good and faithful servant." God is looking for faithful warriors. I fall in love with the idea of giving my best, and then I let God decide what kind of church He wants me to have.

A WINNER FOR GOD

As a young boy, I was a state champion wrestler year after year. I went through a period of my life when I never lost. I wrestled nearly every Saturday and went nearly five years without a loss. I was eleven or twelve years old at the time. From the age of seven, the idea of losing never crossed my path.

One year, I needed to lose two pounds to make my weight class. I was already skin and bones, but to compete I had to lose more weight. My father took me to a health club where I sat in a sauna for what seemed like eternity. The next morning I was tired and weak because I had eaten nothing the day before. But I made the weight.

All day I wrestled match after match until the very end. It was the final match for the state finals, and I was so tired, I could barely stand. The match began, and I had nothing left to give. I lost.

That was one of the hardest days of my life. The other wrestler jumped up in the air with a clenched fist, and the crowd screamed. I stayed on the mat and began to cry. My coach helped me off the mat and encouraged me. He took me to an empty room where I could be alone.

I sat there all by myself, thinking about the match and crying. My father walked into the room, and I didn't know what he would do. Would he be mad? Would he criticize me for not trying harder? He sat next to me and said, "Son, for years I've followed you around the city and watched you wrestle, and you've always won." He put his hand on my shoulder and continued, "As I watched you today I knew that someday you would lose. Today for the first time, I wanted you to lose because I always wanted the chance to show you that I love you no matter what." He said, "You gave your best, and that makes you a champion."

I learned that lesson, and it's with me everywhere I go. God wants me to give my best, and no matter what the results, how many things go wrong, how many things go right, I am a winner for Him.

Some people don't want to think about the pain of being on the losing side. However, others will risk losing for the sake of having a shot at victory. We cannot fear failure, for no one has ever failed who has stayed faithful.

FUEL FOR THE DREAM

After I first arrived in Los Angeles, I started ministering in one of the toughest housing projects in the city. The project was known for its weekly killings, and even movies were made about the Jordan Downs housing project. Now we maintain twenty-six children's church programs in the poorest of the city's neighborhoods.

We were having children's church there one day when a man came up to me with a vicious attitude. He wasn't a gang member or a drug dealer. He was a pastor. He told me that I didn't belong there and that I needed to leave. He was acting as if I were a rival gang member trying to take over his territory. He told me that I wasn't real and that I wouldn't last. Then the hopes of the community would be dashed again. I responded that we had been there more than a year. It didn't matter to him. He believed what he wanted to believe.

He really hurt my feelings. I went behind one of the buildings and started to cry. No way did I want to show my feelings in front of him, but once I was away from everyone, I cried. He took all the wind out of my sails. I thought about what he said, and then I wiped off those tears and continued to minister to the children. Before I left the site I told him, "You have hurt me today, but five years down the road, we will still be here." Five years later, we don't see him anymore, and we are still going strong. Some people fold under criticism. Others rise up and use it as the fuel to accomplish a God-given dream.

The great churches in America have one thing in common—pastors who have persevered over the years. They have been at their churches for decades and have a certain kind of determination to win. In Los Angeles, I'm tested daily, but the testing has made me. Without it I would never grow. I thank that man for saying what he said because God used that to make me better.

MAKE FAILURE YOUR SERVANT

The Old Testament describes King Nebuchadnezzar, who was a wicked king. The things he did to the people of God were so brutal that the very thought of his actions makes me cringe. He was involved in a holocaust, murdering thousands of Jews. He destroyed the temple, the brazen altar, the Holy of Holies, and all of the sacred furnishings of the temple. He also destroyed Jerusalem; his soldiers leveled every house and the walls around the city. His rule was so oppressive that a famine came, and people literally ate their children. This was all caused by the ruthless King Nebuchadnezzar. And yet, God called him His servant.

I can imagine God calling Moses or Abraham His servant, but not Nebuchadnezzar. A man who hated everything about God was called His servant. Why? Because God looked down one day and said something like this: "This wicked king hates Me. This wicked king is trying to destroy My work. This wicked king is trying to destroy Me. This wicked king is trying to destroy My people. I'll show him. I'll make him My servant. I'll take his evil and use it for My good. Nebuchadnezzar thinks he is trying to hurt My people when really he is My servant. He will not hurt My people or Me, and I will see to it that My work is stronger and My people are better. His evil intentions will not destroy My work. They will strengthen the work of God, and I'm going to use his evil intentions for good."

That's what you can do. You can use whatever has come into your life to become your servant. Maybe it's failure or a shattered past. Make it your servant! Maybe it's an enemy or a broken dream. Don't let those moments define who you are. Make them bow down and become your servant. In everything in your life that has come your way to destroy you, turn the tables so that it can benefit you in the future. Make it your servant! God even used wicked people to make His people stronger. The wicked king didn't know it, but he was playing right into the hands of God.

THE POWER TO BELIEVE

In the inner city many young people have heard only negative comments about them. The philosophy is that your dad's a drunk, and you will be too. Most of the people we work with have a failure mentality. They expect to fail before they start something. When I pay them a compliment, they are very slow to receive it because they are not aware of all the good that's inside them.

At our church, we try to restore the power to believe. When someone has been addicted to something for a long time, he has a self-destructive mentality. Whenever he does good, he feels that he can't continue to live that way and falls back to old patterns.

We teach the "new creation" theory. He is a new person, who can start all over again and reprogram new principles of faith in his life. When we have restored a person's ability to believe, we have restored his ability to achieve. We don't spend a lot of time talking about the past. We emphasize the future. We try to destroy the victim mentality and all the excuses why people end up the way they do. We focus on how to overcome obvious weaknesses.

When I was a young evangelist, I was driving with the host pastor of the church where I was speaking. He listed all of his struggles at the church. One by one he let me know everything that was going wrong with the church. He turned to me and said, "The people here are not committed to the church. I can't wait until I get another opportunity to pastor a church where the people will want to do something." Although I was only seventeen and wasn't the wisest person in all the world, something told me that the problem was not the people; it was the pastor's fault.

The people will commit only if they see that the pastor has committed his life to them. If he loved them, bragged on them, shared his vision with them, and asked them to come along, I know they would come along. The secret is to dig your heels into the ground, give it all you've got where God has called you, and don't look back.

I told God that to get me out of Los Angeles, He would have to knock me in the head with a sledgehammer, and then I'd still be fighting. I feel that way because you cannot accomplish your goals without the fierce desire to commit to something with all your heart.

A PRISONER OF HOPE

By all logic, our church should not exist today. We have faced huge financial obstacles. We've needed $4 million in eighteen months to pay off the building. We've had to bring our dilapidated place up to compliance with city codes. We've been down to nothing in our operational account. We've had to reduce our kitchen budget to the point that our residents ate hot dogs every day for a month. During that time, we had many questions and even doubts, but quitting was far from our minds.

Not long after I moved to Los Angeles, some of my friends from Phoenix visited me, and they asked me how long I planned to be there. For some reason, it was hard for them to accept that I regarded LA as my home and my place in the church as my future. Whatever God has called you to do, stand up and say, "I'm going to be faithful and win in my calling." Become a prisoner of hope, and treat your calling with sacred pride every day.

The churches of America need to be filled with the sweet fragrance of hope. When people walk into our churches, they need to feel a sense of expectation that their needs can be met and that their spirits can be lifted, no matter how bad they feel or how low they've gone. That's the kind of energy that flows in our church services. What a joy to look into the choir and band and see lives that have been transformed by the power of God. Why is there so much energy? Because there is a constant flow of new faces. Every Sunday I see changed people singing the praises of God.

At first, I was skeptical that some people could change. I used to think that gang members would always be that way or an addict would always be an addict. However, I don't see life that way anymore. I see every person as someone who is going to be changed. We need to make it a habit to see with the eyes of faith.

A young girl who attended our services was always crying. Although she was only thirteen, she had dated an abusive twenty-five-year-old man. She became pregnant but experienced complications and had a miscarriage. Every week we showed our love to her until she couldn't take it anymore. She accepted Christ and joined our Teen Reach home. Today she talks only about the future—what she wants to be, what her dreams are for life. Everything about her has changed, and her future is bright. People like her throughout the country want to be loved in our local churches.

A NEW DREAM

A new Dream Center is being born in Wilmington, North Carolina. The pastor's name is Rick Stoker. He has been a very successful physician working for some of the finest college basketball teams. At Duke and the University of North Carolina, he has worked in a very professional field with high-caliber athletes. He also visits some of the poorest neighborhoods in Wilmington and gives food to prostitutes, drug addicts, and bridge dwellers.

Rick received calls on his pager from homeless people who were in trouble. He said that they called so often, he had to make a decision in his life about what he was going to do. Many would have thought he would cut back on his hours working with the poor. Instead, he gave up his well-paying job to work with the homeless and start a Dream Center.

I said, "Rick, where are you going to get the money?" He said, "I don't know, but if I have to make a choice between my job and the poor, I'll choose the poor." Rick continues to serve the poor in Wilmington with his own bare hands and he is doing all right.

If you go to Wilmington, look for a man with a big Thermos of soup and a smile. That's Rick. The other day a homeless woman told him, "I sure hope we get our Dream Center because then I can have a mirror to look at myself every morning when I get ready." He told her that the day is near. Rick has decided to be aggressive with life, step out into the unknown, and tear down the devil's kingdom.

What has God called you to do? What is your dream? Once you find out, give your life to it. Don't be afraid of tomorrow. God is already there. In our work for God, let's be like that pitcher. Let's get serious about the work that we are called to do. Let's make every day a masterpiece, and let's strive to be winners and to instill that philosophy into the poor and hurting of our day.

12

Thank You, Sir, for Coming!

I WAS UNPACKING my things and getting settled into my office in Bethel Temple. I received a call from the secretary that a man wanted to talk to me. To be honest, I didn't want to be bothered, and I groaned a little at the thought of talking with him. She said, "Do you want me to tell him to come back later?" I thought about it for a minute but told her to bring him in.

The door opened to reveal a homeless man standing in the doorway. His body smelled of a foul odor, and his clothes were filthy. A ball cap crumpled in the middle rested on his head, and his beard was long and uneven. He looked as if he felt unworthy to be in the office, and he was careful not to sit down on any of the chairs.

We talked a while about the Lord, and I prayed with him a prayer to accept Christ into his heart. I opened my eyes and looked into his. Suddenly like a heavenly vision, the eighth psalm came to my mind:

O LORD our Lord, how excellent is thy name in all the earth! who hast set thy glory above the heavens. Out of the mouth of babes and sucklings hast thou ordained strength because of thine enemies, that thou mightest still the enemy and the avenger. When I consider thy heavens, the work of thy fingers, the moon and the stars, which thou hast ordained; what is man, that thou art mindful of him? and the son of man, that thou visitest him? For thou hast made him a little lower than the angels, and hast crowned him with glory and honor. Thou madest him to have dominion over the works of thy hands; thou hast put all things under his feet. (vv. 1–6 KJV)

God created all things for that man. The Creator of the universe regards him with honor. He made the moon, the stars, and the planets, and He has given dominion over the earth to that man. God made him just a little lower than the angels, and God put all things under his feet. In that moment I realized how important the homeless man was.

When I opened my eyes, his appearance changed. I saw his hair neatly combed, and his pants perfectly pressed. His clothes were new, and he had the sweet smell of a fine fragrance. I stood up and said, "Sir, I want to thank you for blessing me with your presence. I thank you that a man such as you would bless me with your dignity here today." I can still see that man leaving the room, scratching his head a bit and trying to figure out why I was saying all of those nice things to him. That day, I realized that every man, rich or poor, needs to be treated with dignity.

Every person was created with care, given a great name by God, and given power and dominion over the earth. Because he was fearfully and wonderfully made, each man deserves our respect.

TRUE GREATNESS

Greatness is not what great people say about you. Greatness is what ordinary people, who can benefit you nothing, say about you. In our quest to feel significant, we tend to find significance in the wrong places. Everyone wants an endorsement from someone famous, but why not receive an endorsement from a single mother? We frame letters that record what prestigious people say about us. Why not frame a letter from a family that you helped? Some people have been faithful in serving God all of their lives, and their names will never be in lights. But they are some of the greatest people I've ever met. They give so much with little recognition.

At the Dream Center, people from all over America give one year of their lives as missionary volunteers. They live here in a small room, eat in the cafeteria, and raise their own financial support. They give up great jobs and secure salaries to live in the inner city and work. They gain significance by helping other people, and by the time they leave, they will never be the same again. Some people come back a second year.

People become attached to this place and are reluctant

to leave. More than one hundred people volunteer year-round. And Christian people from across the country have moved into the neighborhood to be close to the church. While they are here, they are giving.

We are at our best when we are serving, and it doesn't matter what we have. In all that we do we should treat people with care and concern. That doesn't mean that we are weak; it means that in all we do, we remember the value of each person.

When we counsel someone, we should be concerned about him, his problems, and his future because God created him with high honor. Every person is important, and what we say and how we treat him are important. Positive words have the power to build up people.

My father has never ceased encouraging me. I can't do all things, but I sure believed it when I was growing up. Every day of my life my father told me that he loved me and that I was special. My father believes that we get whatever we brag on. Anyone who knows my father will tell you that he can motivate people as no one else can. Whenever I was discouraged and heartbroken, all I had to do was to give him a call, and he would be there.

Some parents believe that if you brag on your kids too much, it will go to their heads, and they will become arrogant. The opposite is true. Kids who don't receive encouragement from their parents grow up resentful and full of bitterness. Believe me, plenty of things come up in this life to make us humble. A little encouragement is not going to go to anyone's head. My father used to say, "Give someone a pat on the back because everyone's getting a kick in the pants."

One day my father and I were on an elevator, and a father and son joined us on the ride down. My father was in a jolly mood and started talking casually to the man. My father said, "I bet you're as proud of your son as I am of mine." The man looked at my father, then at his son, and said, "I'll tell you later how I feel. I don't want what I say to go to his head." We got off the elevator, and my dad said, "Son, what that man said was very foolish. Don't ever do that." He passed up the chance to show his son how much he loved him.

Why is it so hard for us to tell someone that we love and appreciate him? Maybe we are too concerned about our own burdens to help someone with his burdens. The truth is that healing begins when we help someone else with his burdens. The best therapy is to serve someone in need.

A SERVANT OF THE LORD

We are all familiar with the story of Jim Bakker and the downfall of PTL and his difficulties during the eighties. Jim went through so much pain and suffering that it's a miracle he was able to survive. Not long after he was released from prison, he came to the Dream Center to speak to hurting people while he was still hurting inside.

That night he preached one of the greatest sermons I've ever heard. He spoke of his suffering in prison and all that he lost when he fell. The people at the Dream Center loved him like a brother. He finished preaching and asked my father if he could stay around a couple of days.

He went out into the streets every day. One day he worked with a children's program. One night he ministered to the runaway kids. In fact, he ministered to the throwaway kids literally all night in their house. His heart was connected with the people. He went out into the streets where the homeless lived, and he picked them up for church on the buses. He was a madman for Jesus.

Finally he asked us if he could stay as a volunteer at the center. We agreed, and he became a full-time volunteer at the Dream Center working for free. He painted rooms, counseled kids in the neighborhood, and had a Bible study for some of the residents. Later, he told me that he had been through many healing centers and counseling programs, but they did nothing for him. When he went to the streets and served the poor and ministered to the needy, however, the healing began in his life. I believe that Jim Bakker got on the recovery road when he took his eyes off his problems and started to minister to others.

It's About Others

When people come off the street, they need to learn how to be servants immediately. Many of them have served themselves for so long, a new mentality needs to be inserted. Most of them have been taking for so long that they don't know how to serve. We teach them that it's not about them anymore; it's about others.

For four years I worked as a full-time evangelist. When I went on the road and spoke at other churches, I was amazed at how many programs were for church members and how few programs were for the lost. It was all about *our* recreation, *our* fellowship, and the churches were to minister to the saints. When I gave my altar call, many times no one responded because no one in the service was lost. Many nights I drove home thinking, *What's the point? What am I doing this for? Why not get a job and make some money? What's the use of speaking in churches if there are no unsaved people to preach to?*

Many nights I knocked on the doors of houses surrounding the church and invited people to come to the service at which I was to speak. I wanted someone to be saved. Some people who lived fifty steps from the church didn't even know that a service was being held.

I will never forget one revival in Arizona. The first night sixteen people attended. The future didn't look too bright. I asked church members to go out with me every day at six o'clock, visit homes, and invite people to the revival. All four nights I was the only person who showed up. Before the service I spent two hours knocking on the doors and asking people to hear me preach. I wanted someone to be saved.

Today, I don't have that problem. The people who work here would lay down their lives for the people they love. Some people have been visiting the same block, the same people, every week for three years. We love people in our city. They are not a burden to us but a blessing.

CHRISTIAN LOVE FOR ALL

Not long ago, my father and I were talking to a pastor about ministry. A woman walked out of our church building, and my father's eyes lit up as he started to talk about her. She had lost everything, her family and all, because of drugs, but he told her story with pride. I jumped alongside him and added some aspects to the story that he left out.

The pastor observed, "I have never seen two people more excited about one woman who has nothing to give you, who is only draining your resources by living at the church, and you are talking about her as if she is your biggest giver." We don't get excited about boats, new cars, or financial prosperity. We get excited about changed lives.

One thing is certain: God loves mankind. He holds man in high esteem and places great value on individuals. Jesus always had time for people. He encouraged the woman at the well. He healed one more person although He was tired. When He was on the cross in the middle of His pain, He told John to take care of His mother. Even more amazing, He expressed His care for one man, a thief, dying next to Him on the cross. He told him, "You will be with Me in paradise." What love our Savior had for mankind! What respect He had for man! If Jesus treated us with such dignity that He would die for us, how much more should we show that same dignity to all people in need.

13

GOD HAS A DOGGIE BAG

ONE NIGHT I was at a fancy restaurant with some friends. It had real silver spoons, a piano playing in the background, and waiters dressed to perfection serving the customers. During the dining experience, I saw something that struck me as very funny. A stately woman wearing a beautiful fur coat walked into the restaurant. She was dressed to perfection. She was very elegant and walked like a queen. At dinner, she had the finest table manners and showed what class is really all about. Diamonds sparkled from her finely adorned hand as she ate her meal.

After she finished eating, she did something that I did not expect. She called the waiter over and asked for a doggie bag. The waiter was surprised but honored her request and brought the bag to her. She proceeded to stuff all of the leftovers in the bag. Maybe that's why she was so rich. Although she already had so much, she refused to throw away the leftovers.

NOTHING IS WASTED

That's the way our God is. He is great and powerful, but God has a doggie bag. Our Lord throws nothing away.

Look at the potter making the vessel into something beautiful. However, the vessel that he made of clay was marred in his hand. The faithful potter put the old clump of clay back and started to remake the clay into something.

Our Lord does not give up on anyone. At times He might be like a coach who has to discipline a player by putting him on the bench for a while, but like a good coach, He always puts the player back in the game and gives him a chance to succeed again.

Remember when Jesus fed the five thousand? After He fed all of them including His disciples, Jesus told them to pick up the leftovers. Our God does not allow anything to go to waste. He will use anyone who is willing for His glory.

How many times in the Bible did God use broken vessels to accomplish His plan? When David was in trouble, God used a bunch of renegades who owed money, who were running from the law, who had all kinds of past problems to help David. God used King David after he sinned to continue a great work in gathering the materials for the temple. Rahab the harlot was used greatly in God's plan of deliverance. She came to the aid of the prophets and was honored by God. No matter how far people have gone, if they are willing to come back, God can use them.

BROKEN VESSELS DEDICATED TO GOD

To be honest, most people in our society have some kind of past. Nearly all of my staff members are broken vessels and products of tough circumstances. But God is using them to become great leaders in our day.

One staff member was raised in the housing projects of East Los Angeles where he ran the streets early in his life, a product of a broken home. Another spent nearly a decade of his life in prison because of some things he did on the streets of Oakland before he was saved. Some people who work for God and live at the Dream Center have killed people in the past.

As Christians, we used to think that the only people God could use were kids raised in the church or pastors' kids. But in our day, some of the most effective leaders are those who have tasted the pain of spiritual failure only to rise up and do great things for God. A new generation of broken people, out of the brokenness, is doing incredible things for God.

I believe that the best testimony in the world is not to fall into sin and waste years of your life, but God is using, as never before, broken vessels who feel a sense of gratitude for God's grace and give back to Him with fervor by serving God faithfully. We have the most committed staff in America, and all of them feel that they owe God their lives because He pulled them out of ruts of despair.

I know that we are saved by grace and that we cannot

earn our salvation, but these people act as if they are trying to earn their salvation. Paul said, "That I may win Christ" (Phil. 3:8 KJV). At first, that didn't make sense to me. Why should he have to win Christ when he was the same person who said, "I'm not saved by works; I'm saved by grace"? Paul was conveying this message: "I know that I'm saved by grace through faith, but I'm going to serve God as if I have to earn it. I'm going to work hard every day as if I had to win Christ. I know I have Him, and He lives in me. But out of the gratitude of my heart I will serve Him as if I had to win Him daily." This is the drive that I find in broken people with a desire to serve God.

God's Gift

My personal assistant, Todd, worked in Hollywood for years managing movie theaters. Every Sunday he came to my church, sat there, and regarded me rather skeptically. He seemed to enjoy the services week after week, but he really couldn't figure out why everyone was so excited about Jesus. There was no doubt that he loved the energy of the services, but his understanding was limited to the concept of God. He was raised in a broken family and suffered severe emotional abuse, so it was hard for him to trust others. We talked after church but only in a casual way.

Just a few months after he started attending our church, the congregation left Los Angeles and attended the pastors' school conference in Phoenix, Arizona. Todd knew only a couple of people in the church, but he decided to go along with us anyway. The opening night service was glorious, and a few friends and I were heading for the parking lot when someone noticed that Todd was wandering around the church. Apparently he had no place to stay.

The man with me invited Todd to stay with us at the apartment in Phoenix. We had a wonderful time, and I found Todd to be a very special man. He had issues to work through in his life, but it was apparent that he was searching for significance in his life. I believe that God gave me a gift at that conference in Todd. Immediately he started working for me at the conference by selling tapes and becoming a servant. Soon, he found the Lord and turned to Him with all of his heart.

Those three days changed his life and mine, for both of us realized that God would have us work together. Todd and I have spent many moments together talking about life, where he came from, and the difficulties he's had feeling worthy. Today, he works closer to me than anyone, even my father. He works long hours for virtually nothing.

This man is crazy for God and has lifted the burdens of my life completely off me. His philosophy is that he loves God; that's why he works for Him. He is not trying to prove anything or earn his salvation. He works with all of his might because of his great love for what God has done for him. If I didn't believe in broken vessels and the greatness that lies within them, Todd would not be in my life today. All of those issues that he used to face have faded away, and now he is a powerful force in the work of God and is respected for his organizational work all over America.

FREEING PRISONERS OF THE PAST

In churches all over America broken vessels are ready and willing to work for God if they are given a chance. They will become some of the most loyal people in the world. People come to our church and want to dream again. We have a reputation of turning no one away, regardless of where he has been. Many people start life all over again at the Dream Center.

Many of them might not be pastors, but they know that their gift will be put to use. Everyone has a gift, and if we are wise, we will locate that gift and use it for the kingdom of God.

In too many churches, we hold the past over the heads of people for too long. Many of these people have already been prisoners of the past most of their lives. They need someone who will help them dream again.

A young woman with this problem came to my office to see me. At one time she was involved in a youth group, sang in the choir, and had a bright future in the work of God. She turned away from God for four years, got married, and went through a divorce. Now she is a young mother with a daughter, and she begged me for an opportunity to work in the ministry again. I told her that the old chapter was over with and a new one had begun. We are helping her back on the road to dreaming again. We need to convince people that life is not over because they've had tough times. There is life ahead.

Winning the Fight

I love the sport of boxing. One night I stayed up late to watch some of the regular boxing matches on ESPN. The two fighters were journeymen fighters, which means that neither one was very good. I didn't care. I know that boxing is rough, and it's brutal. But I have to admit that I enjoy watching a good fight.

That night, I tuned into the fight late. One man was pelting his opponent with a flurry of punches, and eventually he knocked his opponent to the floor. The man barely staggered to his feet at the count of eight, the bell rang, and the match was over.

We waited a few minutes for the judges to turn in their scorecards. I thought to myself, *This is going to be easy. We all know who is going to win this fight. Certainly the man who knocked the other man to the ground and won the last round convincingly.* They read the scores, and to my amazement, the man who was beaten badly in the final round won the fight.

The decision made no sense to me. Finally the sports announcer explained the situation: "This fighter lost the last round, but the judges don't declare the winner because of one round. They look at the entire fight before making a decision."

The Lord used that analogy to help me understand life and people. I've learned that in life you can win the fight without winning every round. As Christians, we may judge a person on a few rounds and label them for life, but God doesn't do that. He looks over the entire course of a person's life before He makes His decision. Maybe you've lost a few rounds in your life. Remember that the fight isn't over. Again, you can win the fight without winning every round.

The Bible is full of men who didn't win every round. Look at some of the titles God gave people. He called Noah a preacher of righteousness. We all know that Noah wasn't always a righteous man. Noah was in a drunken stupor after the Flood, and some say that Noah, drunk, exposed himself and possibly committed an immoral act with his son. Noah wasn't always righteous. But God did not look only at that moment in his life when making the decision about what to call him. God looked at all of Noah's life, all of the rounds, and made the determination that he was a preacher of righteousness.

God called Abraham the father of faith. Abraham wasn't always a man of great faith. In fact, he lied and told men of a foreign nation that his wife was his sister. He didn't trust that God would protect him. Several times he did similar things. Yet God declared him the winner after looking at all of his life and called him a father of faith.

God called Moses His servant, the same Moses who struck the rock instead of speaking to it. The same man who was not allowed to enter the promised land because he lacked a servant's heart. And yet God, who looks at all of the chapters of one's life, called him a servant.

God called David a man after God's own heart. But David committed adultery and dishonored a good man with a good name. He was involved in a conspiracy to kill Uriah to cover up his own sin. In fact, David disobeyed all of the Ten Commandments through the course of events with Bathsheba. But in the end, God considered all of David's life, lifted David's hands in victory, and called him a man after God's own heart. What a title given to a man who fell so hard!

Thank God that He sees the finished product. God judges fairly and judges us not only by the bad but also by the good that we try to achieve. Maybe you have great dreams, but you're living in agony because of yesterday. There are still some more rounds left. Win them, learn from your mistakes, and let God declare you a winner.

There are good people with great dreams who are wasting their lives, not because of their sins of yesterday, but because of their refusal to move on and make something of their lives today. The apostle Paul was not a perfect man with a good track record, but he declared, "One thing I do, forgetting those things which are behind and reaching forward to those things which are ahead" (Phil. 3:13 NKJV).

THE GOOD SHEPHERD

I feel that my job in pastoring the church is sometimes like that of being a city janitor. I walk around the city, pick up the shattered glass and broken pieces, and help put them back together. In the inner city I'm surrounded by broken people with no sense of godliness and no sense of what is right or wrong. But these wayward sheep, once they are loved, come home, and they stay forever.

The love of our Lord for His people is truly remarkable. He is the Good Shepherd with only the best interests at heart for His people. All that He does, whether it is to discipline us or encourage us, is to allow us to find true happiness. Jesus said, "I am the good shepherd" (John 10:11 NKJV), and here's why.

The shepherd loves his sheep. He watches carefully over them every day. The sheep are trained to stay together so that the shepherd can keep an eye on them for their own protection. Every once in a while one sheep will stray from the rest. He is too adventurous, and he is easily lured away.

The shepherd continues to try to keep him in the fold, but that one sheep continues to disobey. The shepherd tries to encourage the sheep to stay with the others, but he won't listen. The shepherd loves the sheep and wants what is best for him and wants to protect him. He places the sheep's little leg over his and breaks the leg bone. The sheep shivers in pain as tears roll down the cheeks of the shepherd.

Immediately after he breaks the leg, the shepherd wraps a bandage around the leg of the sheep and carefully cares for him. The sheep doesn't walk like all the others. He has a limp, and it's obvious to all that he has been disciplined. At times the sheep can't keep up with the others because he is injured. The shepherd then takes the sheep in his arms and carries him wherever he goes. He spends much time caring for the sheep and helping him walk again.

One day, the break is healed, and the sheep has learned his lesson and joins the fold. However, it is said that you can always tell which sheep had his leg broken and had to be disciplined because he walks closest to the shepherd. He has a special love for the shepherd.

The good shepherd loves the stray sheep and cares for them and nurses them back to health. In our cities today, let's not forget about the wounded, the hurting, and those who have lost the will to believe. Let's nurse them through recovery and help them dream again. If you do, they will be the ones who won't leave your side. Thank God that He doesn't give up on us, and He doesn't throw us away. He continues to believe in us.

That's what the Dream Center is all about. We teach people to stay in the fold, but if they do stray and have run out of hope and ended up under a bridge, ended up with a needle in a vein, or ended up on the streets in prostitution, we provide care for them. It is said that he who preaches to hurting people will never lack for a crowd. Let's go out, round up all the hurting people, and get them back in the fold for Jesus.

14

CHANGED LIVES

PERHAPS MORE THAN anything else, the stories of changed lives are the best testaments of what God is doing at the Dream Center. Every person has an account of how God has fundamentally changed his life. Yet each story is unique as it chronicles the traumatic events of each life before the individual came to the Dream Center and the miraculous transformation that each person experienced after his arrival here. These testimonies illustrate the need and the fruit of sharing Jesus with others.

BRENDA

My name is Brenda, and I am fourteen years old. I grew up in a family filled with pain and violence. My father beat my mother and dealt drugs. It got so bad, he would even sell and use drugs when our family was at home.

The pain my dad caused my mother made me decide to never marry a man like him. He thought he was showing me and my brother love by giving us money, but all I really wanted was for him to spend time with me.

Time went by, and my father went to jail for selling drugs. He was locked up for three years. While he was in jail, I started getting into trouble, but he got saved.

I didn't know my dad had changed. In fact, I barely knew him anymore. I asked my mom why she stayed with him, and she said she was only doing it for my brother and me.

I began to hang out with a bad crowd. They got me started ditching school and smoking weed. They also took me to a party and introduced me to my first boyfriend. Eventually I fell into what I thought was love and ran away to be with him. I didn't want to be at home because of all of the problems I was having with my mom, and I thought my boyfriend would take care of me.

He told me nothing would happen between us unless I wanted it to happen, but one night I was drunk and he started trying to take advantage of me. He kept trying to mess around and wouldn't stop when I told him to. In the end, he raped me.

In the morning, when I was crying, he told me he did it because he loved me. I felt dirty since I was only eleven and my virginity was important to me. I didn't think anyone would want me anymore.

He convinced me that he was sorry and would never hurt me again, so I stayed with him. Then he got really possessive and started threatening me when I talked to other guys. About a week after he raped me, he started beating me. He said he'd kill me if I left him. Then I ran away from him, but he kept searching for me. Finally he found me at a friend's house and beat me up in front of my friends that were there. I was scared, so after he left, I went home.

A couple of days later I was walking to the store with my little brother when I saw him. He grabbed my brother and told me if I didn't do what he said, he'd take my brother. So I left with him. My dad got out of jail around that time and started looking for me. When he found me, he took me home and tried telling me about the love of God that he had found while he was in jail.

I didn't listen and was soon involved in another bad relationship. My parents sent me to Mexico so I wouldn't end up in another relationship like the last one. My ex-boyfriend killed my new boyfriend a month after I got to Mexico. I ended up staying in Mexico for seven months because my ex-boyfriend was looking for me to kill me.

After I came back, I still wouldn't listen to my parents, so they put me in Teen Reach at the Los Angeles International Church where they were going to church services. In Teen Reach they showed me love and gave me an opportunity and environment in which I was able to grow and change.

Now I know God has a plan for my life and had His hand over me protecting me the whole time. I plan to serve God until the day I die, and I want to help other girls like me.

JOE

One of my first memories was of being switched back and forth between my mom and dad. Both of my parents had remarried after they divorced, so it was like two different families.

My stepmother molested me from when I was two until I turned eight. Since I spent the weekends at my dad's house, it was easy for her to get to me.

Finally, when I was eight, I told my mom that my dad hit me while I was at his house. Later, when she brought the California DA to our house, I told them how my step-mom abused me. Six months later my mom was granted full custody over me.

Even after all of the things I had gone through with my stepmother and dad, I was still brokenhearted when I was no longer allowed to see them. The courts ruled that I would be unable to see my father until I turned eighteen. In my mind, at that point, I couldn't understand why.

The same night the courts ruled in favor of my mom, I told the devil my soul now belonged to him. From that night on, my life was drastically changed.

For four years I went to therapists where I was told I suffered from multiple personalities and attention deficit disorder (ADD). Sometime during that period I began to use drugs, ditch school, smoke cigarettes, and drink.

In my early teenage years I was arrested on various charges around fifteen to twenty times. Some of these charges included petty theft, underage consumption of alcohol, carrying a concealed weapon, drug trafficking, etc. It was only by the grace of God that the majority of these charges were dropped.

When I was fourteen, I was "branded" into a local gang called Rebellious. They took a coat hanger and burned an *R* four inches long and an inch and a half wide into my arm. The scar is still there.

After joining Rebellious my drug usage increased dramatically. In the gang I was expected to jump people in or out, assault random people on the streets, defend the name of the gang, and commit other random acts of violence.

Finally my mom gave up. She was saved at a church service when I was ten, but I never gave Jesus a chance. She never stopped praying for me. One day, somebody told her about a program called Teen Reach at the Los Angeles Dream Center. I would have never gone willingly, so she told me she just wanted me to start going to a new school. I agreed.

When I walked in the door of the school I saw several well-dressed men carrying two-way radios. They looked like cops, so I took off down the street. They chased me through bushes, fences, and bridges. A dog even bit one of them! Then they tackled me and took me back.

That night I entered church not expecting anything, but God had other plans. I don't remember what the service was about, but I found myself weeping at the altar, begging God into my heart.

Now, I am heading up Teen Reach's video production ministry. I'm worshiping God and couldn't be happier! Thank you to everyone who prayed for me and discipled me along the way.

TRACEY

As I walked into the park, the sun shone in my eyes and temporarily blinded me. I could barely see the group of guys I was walking toward. One guy stood out among the rest as he turned and smiled at me. Turning to the girl next to me, I whispered for her to introduce me. I walked up to him and he casually swung an arm around my shoulders and he asked me if I wanted a cigarette. I was almost spellbound by his eyes as he stared at me. His gaze felt like it could almost see into my soul. I accepted the cigarette he handed me and waited for him to light it.

We barely said a word to each other, but it seemed automatic for us to be standing there, in the middle of our friends, with his arm around me. Later, we smoked weed together. As I left I looked up at him as he leaned down to kiss me good night. My stomach did a flip-flop and I didn't want to leave! Softly, so my friends wouldn't hear, he asked me to meet him there again the next day.

It was different the next day. We were with his friends and I was uncomfortable. But as he looked in my eyes, all my doubts fled, and I drank and smoked weed until I loosened up. The next couple of days were like a scene out of a dream world. He bought me everything I wanted and made sure all of his friends knew who, and whose, I was. Then my world crashed.

I was sitting in the living room watching TV when he walked back inside. We had just smoked more weed, so I figured he had been outside smoking another bowl without me. As he came toward me I scooted over to make room for him on the couch, but I looked up and froze. The look of rage on his face shocked me. He slapped me across the face, and pain shot through my neck as my head flew back and I fell off the couch. Standing over me, he asked why I was flirting with other guys.

My mind was numb with shock, and words wouldn't come out, so he slapped me again. Finally I managed to ask him, through my tears, what he was talking about. By then the look was gone and he apologized, but the long relationship of abuse had begun.

Similar situations and much worse occurred for the next two months or so. I strived for perfection so he wouldn't get angry, but nothing worked. Eventually there came a day when I hit the point of no return. The events of this day would affect and haunt me for the rest of my life.

Already high, I showed up at the place he told me to meet him. It was evening, and the sun looked almost bloody as it sank between the mountains. He picked me up in a friend's car and drove me to a house I had never been to. When we got there, he pulled a case of beer out of the backseat, and we went in the house. I looked around and didn't see any other girls except for one standing in the kitchen cleaning. She had long jet-black hair and was pretty except for a purple bruise on the side of her cheek that looked recent. She stared into space as she worked almost as if she didn't even see me when I said hello. So I sat down with a bunch of guys at the table and started drinking.

Probably about an hour and ten beers later, my boyfriend came back in the room. He took one look at me sitting at the table with his friends, and I saw the look of rage in his eyes. He grabbed me by the arm as I stumbled toward a room in the back of the house with three other guys in it.

As soon as we got there, he started beating me. It was worse than the other times, though. When I fell and couldn't get up anymore, he pulled me up by the hair until I was standing, facing him. Then he pulled a gun out from somewhere and held it to the side of my head. I could barely get the words out as I promised him I would never do anything wrong again. Finally, after what seemed like an eternity, he dropped me on the floor, pointed the gun at one of the guys sitting in a chair, and shot him. I covered my eyes and sat there crying as I saw the bullet hit him in the side of the head and his eyes glaze over like glass. Every drop of energy left my body as drops of blood hit me as he slumped in the chair. My mind went blank, and the next thing I remember I was in the bedroom lying down. My clothes had been washed and the girl with black hair was carefully fixing my hair and makeup to cover up the bruises.

In a state of total shock I just closed my eyes and asked her to hand me a pipe and a sack of weed. I lay there and smoked weed until my boyfriend came in to take me back. I saw him several more times after that, and then he skipped town. But his purpose had been achieved. The whole course of my life had been transformed.

Years later, I told my best friend what had happened to me. Until recently, after I got saved, I was unable to even begin talking about it. Today as you read this, you know more than anyone who has ever talked with me on this subject. I could tell you many more traumatic things that have happened since, but this guy, when I was eleven, did more damage to me than every other person combined.

When I came to the Los Angeles Dream Center and Teen Reach, I never thought I would get saved. I had no idea that anyone could or would love me again. I treated the people around me like they were nothing and expected others to do the same to me. But for the first time in my life people loved me unconditionally, no matter how badly I rejected them.

I'm sixteen and only now able to say I am healed. Before when I was filled with bitterness, pain, and anger, I never imagined feeling a joy or peace again. I had lost my innocence, and I knew I couldn't get it back. But by the grace of God I am alive and serving Him today. I am filled with a joy and peace I can't express or describe in words.

From this point on I know whatever happens is God's will. Whether I live or die I will serve Him. No one can take my salvation from me. Thank you, Pastor Matthew, Pastor Tommy, and Pastor Bobby [founder of Teen Reach]. Without people like you I would have given up on myself and life.

LORENA

My name is Lorena, and I am nineteen years of age. I was raised in a broken family. People that I loved very much physically and verbally abused me. At ten years old I fell into drugs and alcohol. I started using crank, weed, drinking alcohol, and using needles now and then. My addiction to crank became really bad. My drug use led to getting kicked out of my school for drug possession.

At eleven years old I overdosed and was placed in a mental institution. It did not help at all. I began getting involved with guys much older than me. I was trying to fill that void inside of me. They would physically abuse me. But I stayed with them.

My addiction increased greatly. People would put me down and tell me I was nothing, was never going to compare to anything in life. I began to believe what they would say. I looked all sucked up and sick. I soon did not care anymore. I began using crack and PCP. The glass pipe became my everything.

I was placed in mental institutions and rehabs almost yearly. Psychiatrists, Narcotics Anonymous (NA), therapists, and various counselors tried helping me. They only helped to a point. Nothing seemed to work. I was too bound to let go. When I first began using, it was just to feel good. Not too much later it was because I had to use to get through the day. I was so hooked I couldn't stop if I wanted to.

Even though I filled my body with all these things I still felt empty and lost. Sometimes I felt like I was going to lose my mind. I always had this concept in my mind that I would die with a glass pipe in my mouth or a gun to my head from my boyfriend.

I overdosed again on a mixture of drugs and medication and almost lost my life. I thought it was over. I was flown to the emergency room, and I began to have many seizures. The doctor said I could die or go into a coma. I almost felt myself drifting away. But I had a praying mom that was not about to lose hope. And God had a plan for me and it was not death.

I came out a week later alive. But I could not walk and I was in a wheelchair. My memory and speech were distorted. God healed me and I can walk again. My memory is back. I know God was just trying to open my eyes, but I still couldn't let go.

I still went back to that glass pipe. I wanted out so bad. It was as if I was locked up in a bottle and couldn't get out. I felt so distant from everything. I started running the streets with my boyfriend. Jumping from town to town.

Living wherever I could lay my head. I got pregnant. But my mind was too far gone to even realize.

I was still being physically abused and was still using. I got so sick, I could barely get out of bed. But that did not stop me. I would lie in bed, still hitting the glass pipe and drinking. It led to me having a miscarriage. It tore me up so bad inside. Sometimes I wanted to die just so that I didn't have to feel all the pain in my life.

A miracle would have to happen for me to be free from drugs. My mom tried everything. And nothing seemed to help. She called Teen Reach. They came and searched and rescued me. They began to minister to me and tell me about the love of God. They told me that God had a calling on my life and I was going to minister to many people's lives. I broke down crying. And I knew that if I didn't give my full 110 percent now to God, then it would be too late tomorrow.

Since then, my life has been completely transformed. I have been set free from the bondage of drugs. The emptiness that I once had has been filled with joy. The love that I was searching for I have found in Jesus. The kind of love that is not counterfeit.

I graduated the Teen Reach program. Now I run a girls' home in Los Angeles, which is full of girls that come from backgrounds similar to mine. I am getting married to a wonderful man of God in two months. I thank God daily for what He has brought me out of, and how far He's going to take me. It had to be a miracle.

KATIE

Walking among the many bodies that were scattered aimlessly on the floor, I walked toward the only light that I could see and entered into a room filled with smoke. Searching to find a small corner to lie down, I looked around and began to recognize some of the faces. The same faces that used to be clearly visible in my mind, but looked as though they were sucked up and distorted because of the endless weeks we had all spent on crank.

As I finally decided to try sleeping for one night, others around me were walking to and from the bathroom doing their drugs. As my best friend, Andrew, put down some of his drugs and stood up, he looked over at me, pulled me to my feet, and took me into the bathroom with another friend. As we climbed over the bloodlessly pale bodies and finally reached the bathroom, he closed and locked the door behind us. Immediately, he pulled out a syringe and began to burn his crank, while the other piled crank in two cut-up straws.

Lucas then took one of the straws, placed it up his nose, and snorted. Andrew leaned over the toilet, put the needle to his vein, and instantly became possessed by the drug he so dearly loved. Then, in a repetitive manner, they handed me the second straw, and although I wanted to sleep, I couldn't turn down the rush of my favorite drug. So I took the straw and snorted the crank.

I could then feel the blood beginning to race through

my body as I realized I would do anything for my high, even if it meant death. But I was unwilling to give up what I knew was my only sense of freedom and continued on. As the blood slowed down, I craved another high. The kind of high that I would only do when society closed its eyes. The blood continued to slow, and my body continued to crave, so I began to take the razor, cut of my own flesh, and drink of my own blood. The blood that I had been tasting of for months now was not enough. I wanted others' blood too. So I took of Andrew's blood after he had tortured his entire arm with an X-acto knife.

Then in a moment's time, I wondered where it all went. Why my life was the way I swore it would never be. I remember swearing as a child that despite how happy those people looked, I would never become one of them. I would never let anything possess me to the point of bondage. As I sat there, my mind began to see my family when we were happy. When we would go to church and take family vacations together. At those thoughts, tears began to roll down my pale face. I wished we could be a family again.

Then I could hear the fighting, the hitting, the screaming, and the cussing all over. I let the fire rise inside of me as I remembered the divorce and what had happened between my family. It hurt. More than any razor cutting you, more than any cigarette burning on your flesh, more than any bondage you could ever be in. It hurt to think about my mom sleeping with any other man than my father. It was a stone wall that I kept on punching over and over.

I didn't know how to get rid of it, so I continued in my lifestyle, taking blood from others and continuing to do crank. I thought it was all God's fault. That He was ruining my family, my dreams, and anything I ever had. So I served Satan. With the blood of others and the knowledge of God, I began to invoke demons. The blood no longer became a craving, but an addiction, and a high in a whole different realm.

Then I finally flipped because of the demons, drugs, and self-mutilation, and was placed in a mental hospital. The same problems arose afterward, so I was then placed into a Christian drug rehab.

Knowing that I needed help, but still serving Satan, I would pray to him every morning. I then decided that I did not want to serve anything or anyone with my 99 percent, so I chose to follow Satan, even though part of me wanted to serve God and change.

On April 25, 1997, I accepted Jesus Christ as my personal Lord and Savior. On that day, He gave me the joy that I've always wanted; to feel like a five-year-old and have my family back. And at that moment, I did. He took all my sin and shame away and washed me clean. He has given me a family of believers and restored broken relationships in my family. He has redeemed me and made me whole. I never thought that I could ever dream again, but He has given me the strength to have dreams and visions. He has also given me a new life and filled me with His joy, His love, and His freedom. I no longer have to be bound to the things of this world, but can rejoice because "He is my tower of refuge and strength."

He has given me my heart's desire and will do the same for you if you serve Him with your 100 percent. Holding nothing back, but giving all the glory and honor to God, "seek ye first the kingdom of God, and his righteousness; and all these things shall be added unto you" (Matt. 6:33 KJV).

ROBBIE

I grew up in a family with a lot of hurt, abuse, and confusion, but I never experienced any of it. My mother and father both remarried after failing in their first marriages. They each had three kids. Three boys and three girls, like the Brady Bunch.

My mother's first marriage was a disaster. She married at the age of seventeen and gave up all she was for him. In the midst of trying to raise a family he would abuse her physically, mentally, and emotionally. Needless to say he was a horrible father. He would twist anything my mother would try to teach her children about God and tell them it was a lie.

Finally my mother got fed up and decided to leave him. Only because she began to fear for the lives of her children. She took the kids and moved on with her life.

My father was extremely depressed at the end of his first marriage. He got to the point where he was sitting in his attic with a loaded shotgun in his hands ready to blow his brains all over the floor. This was while his three children were downstairs playing in the house. Right before he pulled the trigger, Jesus spoke to him about His love and mercy, and right there on the floor of the attic he was radically saved after being backslidden for twenty years.

After my parents got married they had two children. I was the youngest out of eight.

While my mother was pregnant with me she had a leak in her placenta, which caused her to go into labor at about five and a half months. They even brought in a specialty doctor for premature babies because she was *having* this baby. The doctor tried to prepare her for what to expect, having this much of a premature baby. He told her to look away when she was giving birth because it's not a pleasant experience for a mother to watch herself give birth to a dead baby. Then without warning or expectancy, my mother's labor stopped. All of the doctors were stunned. They had never seen anything like it. It was a miracle.

After that whole ordeal, although it was joyful that I lived, the doctors still said that I was going to be premature and have quite a few problems. Praise God, my mom, although she was on her back most of the time, was able to carry me full-term, and I was born as healthy as can be. My mom started calling me "her miracle" and surrendered my life to God, fully knowing that He had something different in store for me. Boy, did He!

As I explained, I wasn't a part of all of the hardship as my brothers and sisters were. I also was the youngest in my family, my oldest sister being fifteen years older than me. So in a way I felt different than the rest of the family. I always just wanted to belong, but I didn't.

One day, when I was seven, I went to my friend's mom's house. His grandpa also lived there and he was an alcoholic. So my friend asked me if I wanted to drink some liquor, and I could tell by the look on his face that he wasn't joking. I immediately said yes and I got drunk for my first time. It was a way for me to fit in. Not only with my friends, but also with my family. I thought maybe if I did the things that adults do, then maybe they'll accept me as a part of the family.

So I was always compelled by acting older than my age just to fit in. At age nine all of my friends were older than me, by two to six years. So when all of them started smoking marijuana at ages twelve through fifteen, I started when I was nine and was immediately condemned to a life full of heartaches, letdowns, and hopelessness.

My mom was totally oblivious to my drug and alcohol use until I was thirteen. By then I was hooked on crank among other drugs, and had experienced things people weren't meant to experience.

My drug addictions grew worse and worse, and I started robbing people to support my habits. I dropped out of school in the eighth grade, and my mom kicked me out of the house, then told the police I was a runaway. I had very little contact with my parents, and every time I tried talking to them, it ended in me cussing them out. To say I was without hope would be an understatement. I was without God.

My mom searched high and low for an answer to my problems. She talked with the district counselor about me, countless numbers of shrinks and psychologists. She even got involved with my school's resource officer. The problem was obvious, but the answer had to be diligently sought.

My mom decided to try some rehab. She got every reference she could, and found every statistic, and looked everywhere for the best. She finally picked the place and had to fork out $16,000 for forty-five days.

So I went and did some rehab. It was the longest forty-five days of my life, and in the end it paid off. I had decided to get myself clean and graduated with honors. Three days later I was getting high again and was back in my ways.

I wanted to get clean but couldn't find the answer I was looking for. I sought after different gods, learned how to meditate, worked the twelve steps, got support from various people, talked over my problems with professionals, and yet still something was missing. I didn't have it within me to change, so I gave up.

Luckily my parents didn't. Both of my parents had fallen away from God, but because of the troubles I had put them through, they fell to their knees. They couldn't stand the thought of losing their son forever. So they went back to what they had learned in the beginning. They went back to what never failed in the past. They remembered that they had an almighty Savior, Deliverer, and Friend who would never leave or forsake them. They got down on their knees and sought after God almighty. They pleaded and begged for forgiveness of their sins, and asked but one thing, that He would save me.

One day while I was at my friend's house the police showed up, and they took me away. I knew I wasn't going to see my friends for a long time, and I told them I'd see them in a couple years. They took me to a holding cell for a couple hours, then they sent me to an emergency placement home. I stayed there for one night, and the only reason I didn't run from there was because there was a very attractive girl who was being very friendly. Whatever the reason I stayed. The next day Pastor Bobby and one other man came and picked me up and shipped me to Phoenix.

It took two months, but on August 11, 1997, I received Jesus and was filled with the Spirit. My life was literally transformed, and I now serve at the Dream Center at age fifteen. I have already graduated high school, and will be starting college in a few months. I know the call of God is on my life, and I will follow Him wherever He leads me. Amen.

JOSE

I grew up in the streets of Oakland. My father was an alcoholic and a drug addict. He beat my mother almost every night.

I found myself going out to the streets at the age of eleven in search of a father figure. Someone to look up to.

I started to drink and smoke weed to fill the void.

I began to miss school. I stopped caring about the things of this world.

I found that there were many of us in the neighborhood going through the same thing. We all knew that we were, but we never talked about it. We just helped each other out without saying much.

When I was fourteen, I started using cocaine and we started a gang. To be initiated, I had to do two things. First, I had to allow every other member of the gang to beat me up. Second, I had to do a drive-by shooting.

I was scared the night of the drive-by. I knew that it was wrong. But I knew that I could not get out of it. I had to do it. I needed a family and love.

I drove up and pulled the trigger. I saw parts of the man's face and body fly off.

That night, my life was changed. Every bit of love and compassion that I had in my heart was gone. After doing that I felt accepted by the gang, and I felt that I belonged.

I was in the gang until I was twenty-eight years old. For

fourteen years, I lived a life of no hope, no purpose, and no future.

I lived by selling drugs. One day, I lost it all. No more house. No more money. No more women. No more friends.

My mother gave me one more chance to live with her as long as I did not do drugs or alcohol.

But I could not stop. One night, she told me, "I want you out of my life. I do not want to have anything to do with you." That night, I felt like I had lost absolutely everything. I felt so alone. I knew that there was a God, but I was not sure if He was real. I cried out to Him to take away the hunger for the alcohol and the drugs. I told Him that if He took it all, I would do whatever He wanted. I cried myself to sleep that night.

The next day, I found a note from my mom telling about a Christian Discipleship House. I gave them a call. They came and picked me up. That day, I accepted Jesus Christ as my Lord and Savior. That was the start of my new life. A new life full of hope and purpose. I now had a future.

About a year ago, the Lord brought me to the Dream Center. I am now studying to be a pastor in the Urban Bible Training College. I am a full-time staff member working in the Spanish Ministry.

One month ago, my father told me that he loved me for the first time in my life. My parents are back together again, and my family is being restored.

I thank God every day for the awesome opportunity to serve Him. I thank Him for my family. I thank Him for my new life. I am a new creature in Christ.

15

He Stood with Them in the Plain

How many times did Jesus feel the need to pray? Can you imagine the pressure that was upon Jesus as He walked this earth? The entire world and the fate of man rested upon this one man. Jesus couldn't be weak as we are. He couldn't slip or make a mistake because He had to be a perfect sacrifice slain for our sins. When Jesus was weak, He always made it a point to go up to the mountains and be with the Father. The strength that He received from talking with the Father allowed Him to carry out His Father's plan.

The more you pour into the lives of others, the more you need to be filled with the power of God. The psalmist said, "I have been anointed with fresh oil" (92:10 NKJV). That's my prayer every day: that I am filled with fresh oil for every new task. My goal is that our church will be not only the busiest outreach church in America but also the most praying church in America.

People sometimes feel that if you're a soul-winning outreach church, you're not a praying church. People try to compare one church as a soul-winning church with another as a praying church. But to be successful, you need two wings of an airplane: outreach and praying. You will crash if you don't have both. Why try to limit yourself? It is possible to have a church where people know how to get on their faces before God and seek Him with all their hearts as well as a church where people get out in the streets and minister to the hurting. I believe we can accomplish both.

THE HEART OF JESUS

In Luke 6:12 (KJV), there is a great lesson about the heart of Jesus: "And it came to pass in those days, that he went out into a mountain to pray, and continued all night in prayer to God." Then in verses 17–18, we read,

And he came down with them, and stood in the plain, and the company of his disciples, and a great multitude of people out of all Judea and Jerusalem, and from the sea coast of Tyre and Sidon, which came to hear him, and to be healed of their diseases; and they that were vexed with unclean spirits: and they were healed.

The passage said that "he came down with them, and stood in the plain." He prayed to the Father all night, and then Jesus came down to where the need was—in the plain. If Jesus hadn't come down to the plain, I wouldn't be here today. If He hadn't come down from the mountaintop, we would all be condemned to hell. But He came down and stood with them in the plain.

"Them" included the common folks, the sick, the poor, the forsaken widows, the orphans, the people with leprosy, the criminals, and the heartbroken. He stood with them in the plain. Jesus said, "My prayer time is up. It's time for Me to go down to the plain. It's time to leave the entourage (the apostles with Him in prayer), and I must go down to where the hurt is." If Jesus had not gone down to the plain, we would not know salvation, redemption, healing, eternal life, or the joy of life as we know it.

There is much said of revival in our land. We feel that if we pray, cry for a while at the altar, invite a group of Christians, and promote the moving of the Spirit, there will be a move of God across the country. But we are recycling the same Christians who are moving from one phenomenon to another.

Revival begins when the heart of the church is touched, and people come down from the mountaintop and stand where the need is—on the plain. This revival will start when the preachers of America come down from the mountaintop and stand with the people in the plain, when churches relate to the common folks, invest their lives in others.

The work every day in the plain is as important as what happens on Sunday morning on the mountaintop. Every Sunday morning I preach to the ministers and encourage them and help them so that during the week they can minister on a daily basis in the community.

Come down, church of America! Come down, pastors, from your fancy sermons and theological concepts, and preach to where the people live. Come down from ritualism to where the hurt is. Come down from lofty explanations of things irrelevant to everyday life to where the pain is. Come down from intellectualism, and help people survive. Churches in Central America and even in Los Angeles put signs outside the door: NO GANG MEMBERS ALLOWED. We need to break down that kind of resistance to helping all people.

SATURDAY ON THE PLAIN

Every Saturday, my father took me to some of the poorest neighborhoods in Phoenix to knock on doors and pick up people for church. The church membership included about four thousand at that time, but every Saturday he picked up people and brought them to church.

My father said to me, "Son, you go this way, I'll go that way, and I'll see you in an hour." I loved those Saturdays with Dad. They taught me about people and about being real as a person.

I do the same thing now but in a different city. I love visiting the children and walking among the people on the plain. Some families won't leave their houses to go to the park until we come by and visit them. The bond with the people is strong, and on my block nearly all of them have come to church.

One boy waits for me every week and calls me the "church man" in Spanish. I go to the next house and visit a little girl we call Pebbles because her hair used to stick straight up. She waits for us, we give her some books and necklaces, and her face lights up. Then we visit Oscar, and he gives us a big hug and a sandwich. You can get fat on the block you have adopted.

I visited Dolores every Saturday for two years before she went back to El Salvador. She got up early every Saturday at 6:00 A.M. and made our visitation team chocolate-covered bananas. It was a special event every Saturday as we ate and played with her grandchildren. She went home to her country, and my heart is still with her.

Walking on the plain and ministering to people unknown to you take courage at first. But after a while, you find yourself excited about meeting people you've never known. My Saturdays are full of joy because I know that I am trying to make somebody's life better.

Some of the situations we encounter are very powerful. Jerry was an older Filipino man who was skin and bones when our team first saw him. He was so weak, he couldn't walk. We ministered to him on his deathbed and prayed for him every Saturday. However, one week we found him walking around his house. Then the next, he was moving around frequently. We prayed for him again, and he started walking up and down the streets. Eventually I saw him a mile from the church walking to McDonald's.

Jerry was being healed right in front of our eyes, gradually progressing every week. We had a great relationship, and I used to tease Jerry by saying, "You're going to live to be two hundred years old. You just won't die."

There is no doubt in my mind that when we minister to people, love them, and care for them, a healing virtue comes upon them. Walking on the plain every Saturday, we are bringing healing to the community.

Christian bookstores sell many books telling us how to stay on the mountaintop. Millions of dollars are being made trying to keep us up there a little bit longer. Evangelists are talking about buying airplanes and prospering. Some are buying enormous houses and fancy cars to show their prosperity. Too many Christians buy books and read them only to find some kind of personal benefit for themselves.

I'm so glad that Jesus had a bigger purpose in life than being concerned about making millions of dollars. I'm so glad that He was more concerned with loving me as a person than winning a preaching award or being famous. I'm thankful that our Lord didn't seek a jet, but instead came as a humble servant to show us how to live. He stood with us, He became one of us, and He visited us on our level. The success that God has given the Dream Center does not come from our big facility or our television ministry. It comes because of the work on the plain.

PROSPERITY IN THE TRUEST SENSE

Sometimes when you minister to others, you have no idea of your impact on them. Every Saturday I visited a woman in her twenties who had just moved to Los Angeles from Honduras. She didn't know anyone except her boyfriend. She was a single mother living with her little boy.

I took candy to her little boy and offered her warm words of encouragement. She was always kind when I spoke to her, but she never really opened up to me as others do when I visit. I basically told her, "I'm here to serve the family and I want to help."

One day, I went to her apartment complex and knocked on the door, but no one was there. I asked a woman walking down the steps where the young woman was. She told me in a matter-of-fact voice that she had died. The story was buzzing around the complex. The previous night, she had been riding in a car with her boyfriend, and they had an argument. He became angry with her and pushed her out of the car while it was moving, crushing her skull upon impact. I couldn't believe it!

A couple of days later, I received a call requesting our chapel and my preaching services for the funeral. I agreed to both.

The day of the funeral, only twenty people were present. On the front row, the mother cried hysterically as I preached the sermon. When it was over, the mother asked me if I was the pastor of the Dream Center. When I nodded my head, she broke down in tears again and said, "My daughter told me about you. My daughter called me and told me, 'There is this nice man who comes every week from the church who gives me such hope.'"

My heart was sinking when she looked me in the eye and said, "You were the only good thing in her life." Moments later she took off her daughter's watch and gave it to me. She said, "I want you to have a part of my daughter. You are a part of our family." All of those weeks, I never knew that I was imparting such hope and spreading such joy to the young woman.

We have to start telling our kids that in this materialistic age, it is truly better to give than to receive. What you gain materially lasts only a season. What you give away to others lasts a lifetime.

I was the speaker at the graduation ceremonies for a Bible college. At the end of my speech a man asked me to tell him my dream. I told him of building a church that never sleeps and pointed out my vision to him, the vision that I've laid out in this book. I then asked, "What is your vision?" He told me that he wanted to have some kids and pastor a church in a nice community. That vision seemed so dull. There has to be more to life than that. Don't misunderstand me; suburban areas need strong churches as much as inner-city neighborhoods do. My concern was that I sensed no fire in his spirit. He just wanted to settle down and be content.

Jesus was the greatest man who ever walked the earth. What would we expect the greatest man who ever lived to be doing on earth? Everything opposite of what Jesus did. That's why we love Him so much today—because we can relate to Jesus. The world tells us that we ought to ascend into greatness, but Jesus teaches us that we are to descend into greatness. The way up is down.

On an airplane I sat next to a pleasant woman who was a teacher in the synagogues of the Jewish faith. She did not believe in Jesus and His authority. We discussed the Bible, and I told her how I loved the Torah and how I've studied the Torah all of my life. She and I talked about stories of the patriarchs in the Bible.

Then we spoke of Jesus. She asked me, "What is it about Jesus that moves people so greatly? What is so special about Jesus?" I told her of how God came down in the form of man, how Jesus didn't come with a great army, but alone with nothing but love for a generation. He could have taken over, but instead He showed us His love by giving His life for us. Rich or poor, people all over the world can relate to Jesus because of His humble, loving, caring servant's heart.

She said, "I just can't see God like that. I can't see Him as a servant." But that's exactly what our God is all about. He sent Jesus to this earth to show us how to live life for another. He came down to the poor, hurting souls and stood with us in the plain.

LOVING THEM ALL

Two eighteen-year-olds in charge of our food truck ministry were delivering food to hundreds of families one day. It had been a long day, and they had worked hard. Driving down the street, they saw the dirtiest homeless man anyone has ever seen. Filth was caked in layers on his hair, and his facial features were barely discernible through the dirt. Obviously he hadn't showered for months.

The two young women stopped the truck, picked up the man, and brought him back to the church. Our people are used to seeing homeless people in all conditions, but he resembled a creature more than a man. The young women took him inside the church with no hesitation, provided him with a shower and clean clothes, then cut his hair. They just went to work on the guy and cleaned him up—no big deal. I told them, "You've been ministering to people for so long, you women are afraid of nothing." When you've been on the plain, you fear nothing. You simply love.

It wouldn't be a bad idea if every Christian in America spent at least three hours a week in the community. If you want to reach your community, find out what is really going on in it. Whether rich or poor, find the needs in your community and meet those needs.

I've heard every excuse why we shouldn't go out into the streets, inner city, or suburbia. People told us door-to-door ministry wouldn't work in Los Angeles because of the city's laid-back mentality. I've learned that love is love, people need it, and we must give it. Let's come down off the mountaintop. Let's expand beyond the walls of our sanctuaries and go out into the plain where the real work is needed.

16

THE BEAUTY OF OUR DREAMS

SOMETIMES WE DON'T REALIZE that we are living the fulfillment of our dreams. We work so hard trying to accomplish something that we fail to see how far we've come. In the pursuit of accomplishing great things for God, we fail to set up monuments along the way in honor of what God has done. In the Bible, people marked as sacred ground the places where God demonstrated Himself or revealed His glory.

One of the great tragedies when we're young is that we may fail to recognize God's provision all along. We get so caught up in trying to reach our destination that we may overlook the importance of the journey on the way to the destination, but the journey is the best part.

GOD'S BLUEPRINTS OF COMPLETION

My mother and I have a very special relationship. Kids called me a momma's boy, and I would have to agree with them. My mother and I talked about life, dreams, what God had for us, every night before we went to bed. She sat on the edge of my bed and proclaimed to me all that she thought I could become.

A couple of times a week we drove down to McDonald's late at night and talked in the car. Those moments were very special to me, and we talked about many things, big and small. Those nights encouraged me to speak my dream as a boy. To my surprise, nearly everything I spoke during those trips to McDonald's has become a reality today.

The beauty of our dreams is that God hears everything that we have to say. He takes note of the things that come from the desires of the heart, and He starts designing His plan of completion the moment that we speak if our motives are pure. We speak things and forget about them, only to see God bring them to completion years later. Many times in ministry I've spoken of things I would like to see done, put them on the shelf for a long time, then one day God allows them to happen.

God hears every pure motive and puts the blueprints of completion together. Every ministry at the Dream Center today was at one time a desire of my heart, and God has done it. I don't become disillusioned if a dream is not fulfilled immediately. If I don't give up, God will allow that dream to reach completion eventually. Too many people give up on a dream right before God brings the fulfillment. Just because a dream is delayed doesn't mean it's denied.

For years, my father preached in cities throughout America. In nearly every big city, he prayed that God would send someone to that city to do a great work for God. Over the years God has honored every request. My father's biggest dream was for Los Angeles. When he was a teenager, he preached throughout southern California and dreamed of a day when he could pastor a church in Los Angeles. He waited forty-five years before God allowed that dream to become a reality. We can't always look at immediate results. We have to take into account God's timing and realize that if we work hard and give it our best, God will allow the dream to come forth.

DYING TO YOUR WILL

The Dream Center is starting a new clinic. It's my biggest dream to have a place where people can receive medical treatment free of charge every day. The county hospitals are full, and many people in the community are illegal immigrants who are afraid of being deported if they seek medical care.

By the time this book is published, one floor will be devoted to medical care for the community. Doctors are coming from all over America to assist the free clinic. This dream has been with me for five years, and the fulfillment is here.

If the dream is God's dream, you have to be willing to

die for it, that is, die to your own will that would hurry things up. Countless times I've had dreams and tried to make them happen—only to fall flat on my face. At other times I kept the dream in the back of my mind and let God bring it about in due season. That's the key, in due season.

The most important thing about a dream is having one. The poorest man in all the world is not the man without a penny to his name. The poorest man is the man who lives without a dream. It is better to have one penny in your pocket and a dream than to have all the money in the world and have no dream. Without a dream we are void of significance.

Some people who volunteer at the Dream Center have a secure job, money in the bank, and a nice home. For a week, they feed the homeless under the bridges, they help the children's ministry, they work in the kitchen, and they minister every day. At the end of the week, they thank me with tears in their eyes. What did I do? Nothing! I worked them hard. They were happy because they stepped out of their comfort zone and did something they had never done before, and that brings joy.

THE EVEREST APPROACH

A famous documentary is called *Everest*. The story is about three people who attempt to do the seemingly impossible, climb Mount Everest. Numerous people have died trying to climb the enormous mountain. Several things can kill you—the avalanches, the cold climate, a wrong step at the wrong time or place. Climbing the mountain requires great skill and wisdom. You can't climb every day and hope to get to the top. If you want the prize of reaching the top, you have to take certain steps. The biggest hurdle is dealing with the thinning of the air as you go higher. You cannot climb thousands of steps a day. You must stop frequently to get used to the new heights. At some points, you have to set up camp, wait there a few days, and do nothing until your body is able to adjust.

The hard part for some people is that they have to stop and set up camp when their desire is to keep moving up the mountain. It's hard for them to focus on how far they've come when all they can see is the glory that lies ahead. But the stopping is mandatory so that they will be able to adjust to new heights and then move forward.

That's the way it is with us. The hardest part of a dream is the waiting. We see the top, the fulfillment, the completion, and the periods in between try our patience. However, these periods make us or break us. God makes us wait so that we can adjust to the new altitudes of our vision.

Thank God that He made me wait for some things, or I would not have been ready to handle them. One by one, in His time, He allowed every dream to be accomplished. He allowed me to adjust as a person while gradually moving toward the dream. I have other dreams for the future, but I must remain patient and steadfast.

Many people in rehabilitation are eager to get their lives back all at once. Immediately they want responsibility and authority. We tell them to take their time because they're not yet ready. We want them to gradually climb up that mountain.

The life of Jesus is the prime example. The last few days of Jesus' life were the hardest of all. The cross, the betrayal of Peter, the agony of death, and the salvation of the world were all on His shoulders. He had the dream of saving mankind, but the hardest steps were the ones closest to the fulfillment.

You may take off fast toward a dream, but then as you get closer, you find out that some of the toughest steps are yet to come. The two hardest things in life are to start and to finish. Many people can't get started on a dream, and others fail to make the final push to finish it.

Some men of God at the end of their lives don't finish strong. Discouragement comes, sin wrecks their lives, they lose sight of the vision, and few make a strong finish. Men of history who became legends for their feats early in life faded off the scene at the end.

My father is determined to finish strong. At sixty-one years of age, he has so much future in his eyes. His ministry has exploded more in his sixties than at any other time in his life. His influence is increasing, and he is as strong as he has ever been. He has always told me, "Son, people will always remember how you finish in life, so finish strong." He has made that final push toward the top of the mountain and is doing more today than he ever has. He enjoys the journey more than the destination.

Our Corporate Dream

The Dream Center is all about helping people reach their dreams. Some people have never had a dream, and we help them find it. Others once had a dream but wasted their lives, so we help them dream again. Some people at our church need to believe in their dream and to be encouraged to stay on the path.

Whoever works at the Dream Center is a part of a corporate dream. We all have individual goals, but we have one main goal and we dream it together: we dream that there will be one area in the city of Los Angeles where everyone in the community will be saved. We dream of a community where children can walk the streets at night and not be fearful of being shot. Our desire is that this community will be the safest in Los Angeles. We have a dream that thousands of people are going out from the church every day, serving people, and spreading hope abroad. We dream of a community of revival, just like that in the book of Acts. Then people from all over the world can look at it and truly know that God can transform any community with willing people ready to serve Him. We might not be a perfect bunch of people, but we believe that God can bless the labor of our hands and sincere hearts.

Wouldn't it be awesome to see the churches of America become the centers of life and activity in our communities? We are doing all that we can to make the church the focal point of people's lives. That's why we do all that we do to reach out.

Together, we work toward that dream with all of our hearts. We plan to open a neighborhood movie theater with good Christian movies for parents and children during the week. We have sports programs where youths can be involved in after-school activities. We offer after-school learning programs and computer training. We even have a bridal shop where people can borrow wedding gowns and tuxedos free of charge.

We have dreams that will last us the rest of our lives. But do we worry? No, because God has already heard our requests and He is working things out according to His timing.

Be Prepared

Pistol Pete Maravich was one of the greatest basketball players of all time. He was a lanky, awkward kid who didn't have much natural talent. He wasn't the kind of player that people could look at and say, "This guy has it together." Pete wanted to be the best in basketball, but realizing his skills were limited, he decided that he would be great at something that very few are great at—dribbling the basketball.

As a teenager, Peter Maravich decided that he would take a basketball with him everywhere he went. If he wanted to be the best, he better learn how to be the best. And he followed through on his plan. It was as if the ball were attached to his hand.

Maravich was so obsessed with playing professional basketball that he was willing to pay the price, and he never lost sight of the dream. When that day came for him to play, he was prepared.

Our job is not to control our destiny. Our job is to be prepared and be the best we can be for God in what He has called us to do. It's His job to prepare the way. Many people have not seen a vision completed because they weren't prepared, and God will wait however long He has to wait until you're prepared. He is not going to give you anything that you can't handle.

TESTS ALONG THE WAY

God is on your side. He is for you and not against you. Will He test you on the road to a dream? Yes! I have found that whenever you set out to do something for God, some of the biggest tests will come in the first year.

Quit giving the devil credit for the trials. God allows

them to come to make you stronger so that you can pass future tests. Sometimes God will put the biggest tests in your way early on to see immediately what you are made of. Every time you pass one more test, you gain more strength, and your faith grows. The more you pass, the more faith you have, and the easier it is to deal with future struggles.

King David was anointed as a young boy. You know the story. Samuel went to choose a king from David's father's house. But none of the sons were the one the prophet Samuel was looking for. Samuel asked Jesse if he had any more sons, and Jesse told him that David was out working among the sheep. Jesse was told to bring him in, and David was chosen to be the king. I'm sure that David was surprised to be a shepherd boy one minute and a king the next.

However, he didn't receive authority to be king until years down the road. David went back to his job as a shepherd. It was the most important time of David's life. He had already been anointed, and one day he would be appointed. The dream was right in front of David, but he had to stay faithful between the anointing and the appointing.

Like David, please stay focused because one day you will be appointed. Don't do anything to ruin your chances. Keep your faith; don't lose heart.

God, the Architect of your dreams, has great things in store for you. Hold on to the dreams. You have been anointed, and you have an appointment out there. Enjoy the journey, and watch God take care of all your dreams and desires: "Seek ye first the kingdom of God, and his righteousness; and all these things shall be added unto you" (Matt. 6:33 KJV).

17

The Desires of Your Heart

While I was working hard at the church late one night, a woman in the church expressed her concern to me, "Pastor, I'm worried that you are growing up too fast. You need time to be young. You are too young to have all of these pressures."

I thought about it for a while and thought of all my friends back home who were having a great time, enjoying life, living in comfort with not much demand on their lives. For a second, I entertained the thought of living the way they lived. It was easier than what I was doing.

She continued, "You are too young to be a pastor of a church."

Questions raced through my mind: *Am I too young? Can I do this? Am I wasting many years of my life chasing after a dream? Will this affect my social life? Will I ever have a chance to be young again?*

That wasn't the first time I had thought about the subject. Throughout my early twenties, I asked myself, Am I missing out on something? Sometimes, I wanted to quit along the way, but when you attach yourself to people and a community that you love, it's very hard to break free.

ESTABLISHING PRIORITIES

There is much discussion in the church today regarding priorities. We make little lists and try to put in order what's most important and what's least important, for example, God first, family second, job third, church fourth, and so on.

But I believe that God is number one, your family is number one, your job is number one, and attending church is number one. The Bible says, "Whatsoever thy hand findeth to do, do it with thy might" (Eccl. 9:10 KJV). Everything should be number one, and you should give your best to all that you do. When it's time to work, give it your best. When it's time to be with your family, give your family your best. Whatever you are doing at the moment is the most important thing in your life.

My father was away from home a lot, preaching on the road, when I was younger, but I was never angry with him for being gone. Some pastors' kids tend to blame things on their fathers because they were busy preaching, but I tend to believe that most of the blame needs to rest upon the kids. They often pass the blame on to their fathers or mothers because they have failed to measure up personally. Sure, my dad was gone a lot, but whenever he had the chance to be with me, he put all of his heart and soul into the time we spent together.

Even though he was busy I respected the fact that he had a dream, a goal, and a world he wanted to touch, yet he did all he could as a father to show me his love. I've never despised my father for chasing after a God-given dream. My father has always loved me more than any son could be loved, but at the same time his love for God was greater than his love for me and I respected that.

THE BEST YEARS

We may worry about the things that we sacrifice when we follow God's will. Instead, we should think about all the things we would miss if we didn't follow His will. The things we give up are far less than the things we gain when we step out and achieve God's plan. He gives us more than we could ever imagine.

To be honest, I thought hard about what that woman said. Basically she told me, "Why are you giving the best years of your life to becoming a pastor?" Then I realized, thank God, that I am giving God the best years of my life. Praise God, I don't have to wait until I've lost everything to finally decide to serve Him. I am going to serve Him while I'm young and can give Him my best.

Actors and sports stars tend to give their lives to God after they've lost it all, after they have no more influence, after their names are no longer on marquees. Thanks be to

God, they come to Him, but too often they come with empty hands to lay at the feet of the Master. I realized that giving Him my all right now was the best thing I could ever do with my life.

That realization changed everything for me. I recognized that by serving God, I was gaining it all. Every day serving God was chalking up another victory in my life. At the age of twenty I could already make a difference in the world. Much of the focus of the younger generation is on *me:* What will *I* become? What will *I* acquire? What will *I* gain? It wasn't about *me* anymore. It was about *we*—my God and me together doing His will. As a result, my life is beautiful. Sure I've been through trials that many people won't go through, my life has been threatened more than once, and yes, I've been lonely. But looking back, I cannot compare the difficulties to the victories.

We, as people, were made for struggle. We are not truly fulfilled when things are going perfectly. We require a struggle. For example, a man will go to a gym, work his body, and lift a heavy bar weighing hundreds of pounds. He will groan and push until he lifts that bar. We call that lifting weights. We call that fulfilling. It's fulfilling because he created a struggle for himself.

When you take care of God's will, He will take care of you. In the volunteer program at our church the people receive no salary, and they work every day in our street ministries. Sometimes I feel bad for them because they have no money and have to struggle for the year of their service. I know that's all part of the commitment, but my heart goes out to them.

For two years, I received no salary working in the church as the pastor. I did that so that I could relate to what the other people go through. I wanted to know what it was like to really live by faith and trust God. During that time, I received a tidal wave of blessings. The year-end offerings were bigger during those two years when I received no salary than now when I do receive one.

The love of our God for His committed soldiers is incredible. Young people, don't spend your lives worrying about what you will do, what you will be, what you will accomplish. Wait for Him and He will supply all that you need. God will take care of every need if you put Him first.

THE WOMAN OF MY DREAMS

Now back to the story that I told you many pages ago I would finish. As the pastor of the Los Angeles International Church (the Dream Center), I found it hard to date young women. Every eye is on me as the senior pastor, and every move is analyzed. Dating possibilities were very limited for five years, and I didn't think I would ever have the time to find a woman to share my life with.

You remember that beautiful young woman I mentioned earlier who feeds thousands of people in the streets of Los Angeles? Her name is Caroline. Well, more than just her work for God impressed me. I was intrigued by her as a person, and I wanted to take her out on a date. To be honest, I was scared to ask her.

We spoke often in my office about the food ministry. She was always pleasant as she told me all the good things. But we seldom had the opportunity to talk about other things. One day I found the courage to ask her out, and she said yes.

Our first date was a trip to Disneyland. That night, I knew that Caroline was the one for my life. I couldn't sleep, thinking of her. My head was spinning and my world was turned upside down. For the next few months we dated and had fun together.

One night we were roller-skating and having a great time. We were approaching our final lap when a man ran into her and knocked her to the floor. She fell facedown. She was knocked out and had a giant bump on her head the size of a baseball. Within a few minutes she was able to speak, but none of the words made any sense. Very concerned, I picked her up and took her outside to the parking lot. My heart was beating fast because I was worried that something serious had happened to her. To keep her awake, I asked her many questions, and she responded but could not recognize who I was or what was going on.

I was ready to drive her to the hospital when she collapsed in front of the car. Then I realized she needed instant help. A woman nearby called the paramedics. By the time they reached us, I had Caroline's head lying in my lap. I was gently stroking her pretty blonde hair and speaking to her so she didn't fade out of consciousness.

The paramedics checked her pulse and her head and asked her familiar questions, "What's your name? How old are you?" She answered the questions, but was unable to do much more than that. Then a paramedic turned to me, pointed, and said, "Do you know who this man is?" All of a sudden, she turned her head, and a big smile spread across her face as she said, "Yes, he's the man of my dreams." Those big, tough paramedics let out an "ahhhh." I looked at the paramedics and said, "Guys, I think she's okay."

Months went by, and I *knew* that she was the woman of my dreams. She had been raised in Los Angeles, but she had a dream of going to New York City and visiting the Empire State Building. She had traveled only through California and Arizona, so I listened to all of her dreams. Every man in love ought to listen for the little things that a woman says and try to meet her needs and make her feel special.

Our family was going to New York in June for a family vacation. We hadn't taken one for more than five years, and we were all excited about it. But I wanted Caroline to be there too. My father gave me some extra Frequent Flyer miles, so I planned to surprise Caroline with the trip.

I called Bill Wilson, a friend in New York City, and we

conceived a little plan to make Caroline think she was going to speak at Bill's church in the city. He arranged it perfectly. He sent her a professional letter from his church asking her to speak to his staff members about her ministry. His secretary called and confirmed the engagement.

Caroline was excited about going to New York to speak and seeing some of the sights. I told her how happy I was for her, but in my heart I wanted to laugh. We carried off the plan for one month without giving away the surprise. She even contacted all of the food banks in New York and got them set up to receive more food, as she does here in Los Angeles.

The day came for her to fly to New York. She left at 6:50 A.M. She didn't realize it, but I left at 5:20 the same morning on another flight. She arrived, and a woman met her at the gate (who was a part of the scheme) and told her that she was going to take her into the big city for one night before they had to get to work in the morning.

The woman took Caroline to the top of the Empire State Building, and for a few minutes she gazed at the skyline. Out of the blue, I came up behind her and tapped her on the shoulder. She turned around, and she almost fainted. I had been waiting for an hour on top of that building. It was the longest wait of my life.

I took her by the hand and led her to the part of the building that had the best view of the city. I was nervous, but I managed to say, "May I have your attention please?"

The area was packed with onlookers, and all of them looked at me. I continued, "I want you all to know that I love this woman with all of my heart, and I flew all the way from Los Angeles to let her know that she is the one that I want to spend the rest of my life with." I got down on one knee, presented the ring, and said, "Caroline, will you marry me?" She said, "Yes," and everyone cheered. We hugged for what seemed like an eternity.

That night we had dinner with my parents at the Boathouse restaurant in Central Park and celebrated the engagement. The rest of the week we celebrated in New York City with my family.

But there was more. We were walking down Madison Avenue, and my mom, sister, and Caroline had to go shopping at the famous Saks Fifth Avenue. In the store, they found the most beautiful wedding dress that they had ever seen. Caroline tried it on, and it was the dress of her dreams. The only problem was that she couldn't afford it and I couldn't afford it. We put the idea aside as a fantasy. However, my brother-in-law, who was with us, went back to the store, bought the wedding dress for Caroline, and presented it to her. I could not believe it, and neither could she.

The week was like a dream come true for all of us. A free trip, an engagement, a wedding dress, and we were two inner-city workers having the time of our lives livin' large in New York City.

A Very Bright and God-Directed Future

Caroline and I have been married for a few months. We are going to have a great life together. We love each other as much as two human beings can love each other, but more important, we love God and the ones that He loves, including the poor and the hurting. I had been concerned about whether I could find a wife with the same concerns and desires, but did God ever supply me with a great wife and a great future.

God takes care of His people. Yes, the work of God takes sacrifice, commitment, struggles, and pain. But at the same time, doing His work provides the greatest joy anyone could ever know. What do you lose by serving God and giving Him all you've got? Nothing! What do you gain by serving God and giving Him all you've got? Everything! Don't be afraid to step out into the unknown. Don't be afraid to have your life radically altered. Great blessings are there, but you have to believe and set your face toward the promises.

The Dream Center is moving forward with complete trust in God. Every day of our lives those of us at the Dream Center wake up with the hope that this country can be changed. God has answered every cry of our hearts and wiped every tear. How many times have we cried from the depths of our hearts only to see God show up one more time with one more miracle?

Our cities are hurting. They are in need of a loving

touch from willing vessels who are not afraid to lay down their lives for a nation that is falling apart. Will you pay the price? Will you wipe the tears from the eyes of a little boy who has no dad or a girl who has been abused mentally and sexually? Will you change the destiny of a city by loving one soul at a time?

We have lived in a great day, and we have seen the hand of God upon one of the great cities of the world, the City of Angels. We know we have more work to do, but our God is with us.

When we lay down our lives and realize that this is not our work but God's, we rest in assurance that everything is going to be all right. Do we worry? Sometimes, but it's getting harder to worry when we have seen a pattern of God's faithfulness over the last five years. The best place and the safest place we could ever be is in the will of God.

I'm safer here than in Orange County or any suburban community because I'm in the center of God's will, the only place to be. God has honored every desire of my life because I honored the desire of His heart to help the hurting and to seek the welfare of the people.

Many people ask me, "What is the future of the Dream Center? What lies ahead?" To be honest, I can't answer them. I'll just take a walk around the neighborhood and listen to the cries of the people, and then I'll seek a solution to quiet those tears. When I find a solution, I'll find more cries and more solutions. But I do know that no demon of hell can pull me away from the inner city and these precious people that I dearly love.

At the Dream Center we will continue to minister to the prostitutes. We will continue to go to the same streets and tell the homeless there is hope. We will tell the single mother that God loves her and has a plan for her life. We will march down the streets of Hollywood with the big cross pointing people to the Savior. The buses will still roll to the projects, and little kids will come to church to enjoy a couple of hours away from the hell they call home. The Dream Center will still be here on the top of the hill, lives will continue to be changed, and the doors will be open day and night for all who need hope because we are "the church that never sleeps."

About the Author

Matthew Barnett grew up in one of the most dynamic churches in America. He daily observed the inner workings of one of the largest churches in the country, Phoenix First Assembly.

As a youth, Matthew was active in many outreaches, and as a young teenager he led a group each Friday night to Mill Avenue near the campus of Arizona State University. There Matthew would counsel college students who were dealing with life's problems.

Fittingly enough, at age sixteen his first preaching experience took place at Church on the Street. Located in the heart of Phoenix's inner city, Church on the Street was a perfect starting point for Matthew. That night he touched the audience, and several came to the altar for prayer. Matthew continued preaching all around America and throughout the world. His heart, however, was in the inner city. Eventually, the opportunity arose to join his father, Tommy Barnett, to reach the lost and hurting in Los Angeles.

Today, Matthew works full-time at the Dream Center and leads the daily charge to help those in need. He oversees more than ten ethnic groups that meet weekly at the Dream Center and 180 outreaches that exist to help the hurting. His passion and energy are contagious. He preaches up to four different services a week, leads the staff and volunteers into uncharted ministries, and shows how to extend a loving heart to all.